# BEGINNING TO PLAY

## Debating Play Series

Series Editor: Tina Bruce

The intention behind the Debating Play series is to encourage readers to reflect on their practice so that they are in a position to offer high quality play opportunities to children. The series will help those working with young children and their families in diverse ways and contexts, to think about how to cultivate early childhood play with rich learning potential.

The *Debating Play* series examines cultural myths and taboos. It considers matters of human rights and progress towards inclusion in the right to play for children with complex needs. It looks at time honoured practices and argues for the removal of constraints on emergent play. It challenges readers to be committed to promoting play opportunities for children traumatised through war, flight, violence and separation from loved ones. The series draws upon crucial contemporary research which demonstrates how children in different parts of the world develop their own play culture in ways which help them to make sense of their lives.

*Published and forthcoming titles*

Holland: *We Don't Play With Guns Here*
Hyder: *War, Conflict and Play*
Kalliala: *Play Culture in a Changing World*
Manning-Morton: *A Time to Play: Playing, growing and learning in the first three years of life*
Orr: *My Right to Play: A Child with Complex Needs*

# BEGINNING TO PLAY

## Young children from birth to three

## Ruth Forbes

Open University Press

Open University Press
McGraw-Hill Education
McGraw-Hill House
Shoppenhangers Road
Maidenhead
Berkshire
England
SL6 2QL

email: enquiries@openup.co.uk
world wide web: www.openup.co.uk

and Two Penn Plaza, New York, NY 10121-2289, USA

First published 2004

A catalogue record of this book is available from the British Library

ISBN 0 335 21431 2 (pb) 0 335 21432 0 (hb)

Library of Congress Cataloging-in-Publication Data
CIP data applied for

Typeset by YHT Ltd, London
Printed in the UK by Bell & Bain Ltd, Glasgow

# CONTENTS

# SERIES EDITOR'S PREFACE

The Debating Play series is not intended to make comfortable reading. This is because 'play' is not a comfortable subject. For a century at least, play has been hotly debated among researchers, practitioners, parents, politicians and policy makers. Arguments have centred around whether it should have a place in any childhood curriculum framework. Its presence in schools and other institutions and settings has ebbed and flowed according to who holds power, influence and authority to control curriculum decisions. When play has been permitted in settings, it has often suffered from a work/play divide. Play in such contexts is frequently confused with recreation. However, an alternative approach is to offer 'free play', through which children are thought to learn naturally. This works well in mixed age groups (2–7 years) when older, more experienced child players act as tutors and initiate younger children, helping them to learn through their play. Sadly, though, this is rarely experienced in early childhood settings in the UK nowadays. It is noteworthy, however, that a few nursery schools have managed, against great odds, to keep an age range from 3–5 years. Research (Siraj-Blatchford *et al.* 2002) indicates that the learning that children do through their play in these settings is rich. There is a growing understanding of the importance of play as diverse evidence accrues, which highlights the role of play in early learning in relation to ideas, feelings, relationships and movement (embodiment). However, this is often mistakenly interpreted as adults showing children how to play, through guiding, tutoring, role-modelling or whatever name is of current fashion, rather than providing children with genuine opportunities to engage in their *own* play.

The Debating Play series is evidence based rather than belief driven, and each book probes an aspect of play.

Ruth Forbes has, for many years, worked closely with Elinor Goldschmeid, who pioneered 'treasure baskets' for sitting babies, and 'heuristic play' for toddlers. This has given her a strong base from which to develop her work with babies and toddlers.

Her current work, continues in this tradition valuing careful observation, informed and influenced by knowledge and understanding of how children develop, sensitivity to young children, and respect which embraces inclusion and diversity. However, her work is evidence based , and is currently helping students, practitioners, parents and carers to develop ways of relating and interacting with the youngest children with great quality in ways appropriate for home and group care settings at a time of great expansion.

The important messages in this book will help those who spend time with and love children to deepen the quality of what they offer to children and their families.

Professor Tina Bruce

# ACKNOWLEDGEMENTS

The idea for this book arose during my studies for a master's degree in Early Childhood Education with Care. There I was privileged to be part of a group of educators who debated, discussed and played over a deliciously rich period of three years. We played and learned together – at making dens and camping out (some of us), re-visiting Piaget through mime and dance. We free-flowed while we continued with our home and family lives, busy working in and supporting services in a range of early years settings, writing, singing, making close friendships and relationships, where today still close attachments are maintained and treasured. Thank you to Tina, Margy, Colin and particularly Patrick, my dissertation tutor, for your support over those three years. I had never contemplated being 'a writer' and I think I know now how a child feels when they are in that possible alternative world of 'as if', having been lifted to the highest level of functioning.

Thanks and acknowledgement must go to all the practitioners, parents, babies and children I have had the pleasure of knowing over the last 20 years in a range of settings. Thanks to the following babies and their families for permission for photographs and sharing the treasure basket video diaries: Mr and Mrs R.M. Oelmann and Elizabeth for the 'what is this?' photographs; Colin and Debbie Robson and George for the treasure basket observation and photograph (copyright © Kip Hambis at MHP Photos); and Andy and Sam Adams and Niamh for the photograph of 'tongue poking'. Special thanks go to the following for taking part in and sharing the treasure basket research, video diary and photographs: Fiona and Dale Smith and Cerys, Jason and Kirsten Skinner and Harry, and Nicola and Derek Thompson and Alice.

Thanks to colleagues at Jigsaw, especially Sam Adams, Sally

Gostling and the baby room team at Broome for their patience and flexibility as I filmed and observed, and for the discussions and debates we had about babies beginning to play ... inspiring and challenging, thank you, it was so much fun.

Special thanks go to Tina Bruce, without whom this book would never have been written. Her faith and trust in me as a new writer has been implicit. Her quiet, constructive feedback and encouragement as a 'critical friend' anchored and kept me afloat.

Thank you to my family, who I have not had quite so much time to play with. To Ian, Alistair and Laura for the emotional and nutritional sustenance, and the need for quiet time and space respected. Finally, to my mother Norah, whose love and pride in all our achievements are as strong today as when I was beginning to play. Thank you to her and my father for a really rich childhood of imaginative play opportunities, and those passed on to their grandchildren.

Ruth Forbes

# FOREWORD

The closer you get to babies, the more complex they become; there is a general opinion that anyone can work with babies, when in reality this is not so.

When as a patient awaiting treatment for a hip replacement, the consultant appeared with his retinue of junior doctors, medical students, nurses, etc., and said to the assembled audience, 'I will see the limb on Thursday', to which I responded, 'Shall I come too?' How many times have we observed adults talking over the heads of babies and toddlers? Or heard nursery staff say that working with babies is uninteresting and not what they really trained to do?

Babies need adults who understand and can respond to the complexity of their rapid development in the first year. What an exciting time it must be to the baby, seeing the world as it appears and hearing sounds never before encountered. Then that momentous occasion when the world looks so different from that viewed previously from a prone position. How different everything and everyone looks when the baby can sit or stands for a few moments. And babies need the adult who cares for them to be animated and celebrate this with them.

We do, of course, as caring and responsible adults, have to make decisions for them or offer them safe choices. As we begin to learn more about babies' complex levels of understanding and their early ability to communicate, there have to be ways of including them in the options that are being offered around them. The way in which we communicate to baby that it is time to change his nappy or clothes, or to move him to another area of the room, whether in a nursery or at home, these seemingly simple moments are key in a baby's day.

In an out-of-home setting, the gestures and language skills we, as adults caring for other people's babies, develop are crucial. Just as important are the skills of caring for and getting to know the baby's family, essential in a relationship or triangle of care.

Now in the increasingly stressful twenty-first century, it is crucial that practitioners hold on to the key needs of very young babies and children, ensuring that their emotional development is supported in a warm, unhurried manner. This is a time for touching, holding, speaking and listening to the baby, which must be both planned for and supported in an out-of-home setting.

This is what is important. Contented babies beginning to play and adults creating an environment in which it is recognized that very young babies have the right to have interesting people and objects around them. This will support babies' need to explore the things that they are interested in and, as they begin to try things out, then we will *really see babies beginning to play*.

Over the last few years, Ruth and I have had many stimulating discussions around the play of babies and adults. This book does not claim to have all of the answers, but seeks to challenge early years staff to start to look at and respond to babies as they begin to play. Enjoy playing with the babies you care for, and never underestimate the value of the time you spend talking, listening, watching and responding to their play.

Elinor Goldschmied
Sept 02

# 1

# ANCHOR POINTS IN THE FIRST YEAR

*Anchors are about enabling the meeting, greeting and sustaining aspects of life. Anchors are about balance and stability. They keep a ship stable in dock while repairs are being made. New crew come on board and then the anchor is raised to enable the ship to move on to a new voyage, to meet new challenges, enjoy new experiences. Anchor points are crucial and throughout this book we will return and revisit those anchors.*

## Why anchors are necessary

Most adults have someone or something providing a point of security or support. It might be a person, the friend we phone at 4 am when the world appears to be turning upside down. Or it could be a place we go to for contemplation or gather some sort of physical comfort – the kitchen we grew up in with its familiar smells or an old, comfortable chair.

One of my anchors was the place where my late father used to sit, on the top of a hill, taking in the views of the rolling Wiltshire countryside. I could, for a long time, feel his presence there and used to have conversations that invariably started with 'Why . . . ?' He had been my anchor; and very suddenly, the huge (in the psychological sense) supporting, loving figure had gone. I hadn't had the chance to say 'goodbye' and, as time passed, I experienced all the emotions of him not being there, to share in my new experiences, my pregnancies and the subsequent greeting of our own babies, new homes, career changes, sharing a family tea party and our babies' first steps.

For babies and very young children, anchor points are crucial, particularly when we think about their development and the beginnings of play. Those with the responsibility for caring for and educating other people's babies become part of the anchorage system. The work of Elfer (1996), Goldschmied and Selleck (1996) and Rutter (1981), demonstrates that secure attachment and separation relationships are crucial in early life. The denial of close personal relationships in group settings is something those in the position of managing and organizing group settings forget at the peril of later development. (Goldschmied personal communication)

## Being someone's anchor

A huge part of the skill of working with other people's babies is knowing when to let the anchor down and when to haul it up. It is a tricky business! Let the anchor down too soon and the baby has no experience of struggle; let the anchor down too late and the baby becomes distressed. If you are looking after several children in a group setting, it becomes trickier.

Goleman's (1996) work has helped us consider emotional literacy and the capacity to feel positive about oneself. He emphasizes the importance of having a high level of self-esteem and being able to think about our own feelings and behaviour as well as those of other people. Only then does play begin. These skills need to be learnt very early on in life and are the areas that a supportive framework for working with children from birth to 3 years must focus on. As Goleman has observed, the ability to handle feelings and emotions successfully may be more significant than IQ in terms of a child's long-term attainment.

## Anchors for practice

In the twenty-first century, we are beginning to see from the work of neuroscientists and researchers such as Blakemore (1998) and Greenfield (1999) that the first three years are critical. The experiences of the developing foetus and the first year of a baby's life are crucial and formative, having an impact on the building of the brain. The way babies develop their play is part of this process. Many scientists and researchers agree that the first three years are of vital importance in terms of the young child's experiences, how nature and nurture interact and the effect on our adult life.

For many years, early years programmes, curriculum development, early childhood studies courses, childcare courses and training have focused mainly on children in the 3 to 5 age group. Selleck & Griffin

(1996) reminds us of the importance of the very early years, since practitioners working with very young children, together with parents, are partners in building solid foundations. Practitioners in a range of out-of-home settings will support young children to build and experience strong and secure emotional attachments with a few close adults if they are to develop play. This will ensure that as the child moves within a setting, they are able to develop and maintain relationships with a new key person and for their play to develop. Post and Hohmann (2000) describe systems in which babies and practitioners move together in the setting through the infant and toddler age groups. In all settings, practitioners need to debate and explore ways of introducing the key-person approach and managing children's moves just as they debate and discuss the play needs and issues of those children.

## Play begins at birth

Practitioners seeking guidance and advice on appropriate material for developing early play for very young children often look to North America, Australia or New Zealand for material written about the birth to 3s age group. The National Association for the Education of Young Children (NAEYC) in Washington advises the practitioners that a curriculum for children under 2 should not be a 'watered down version of the older child's curriculum'. For too long, curriculum development, childcare courses and early years practitioners have focused on the 3 to 5 age group.

Penn (1999) notes that much of the original guidance of the NAEYC arose from the work of developmental psychologists, using checklists to advise practitioners on environment, activities and learning opportunities. It lists the skills required by adults working with other people's children in the USA. The book has been used as a basis for practitioner training and assessment of skill levels. Penn considers this checkpoint approach an inappropriate measure of practitioner learning and of the level of quality that a setting provides.

The emphasis on checklists was part of the US government's programme to improve the quality of childcare provision through more stringent registration requirements. Research in the USA by Cryer and Burchinal (1997) supported theories that parents' definitions of quality were different to those of trained childcare observers and were uninformed about the important contribution play makes to the development of learning. Chris Athey (1990), working with Bruce, also observed that parents and childcare professionals have issues about understanding and agreeing on such aspects as play, individuality and creativity and the way parents have grown in confidence and knowledge through discussion of how their children play at home and in the centre.

## The problem of looking at 'milestones' in the development of play ▋

After seeing how heuristic play has affected provision for the young children under 3 in her day nursery, Holland (1997) has challenged the use of, and over-reliance on, developmental checklists. The 'milestone' approach can cause concern for parents and practitioners if children are not 'at' a milestone or the emphasis is on moving the child 'on' to the next stage, whether or not it is relevant or appropriate for that child. While working with children under 2, I have become more aware of the pressure both on and by parents; for example requests for the setting to introduce 'proper' reading to the under 2s, and for a child to 'move up' to the next group (Forbes 1999a) where the parent perceives there to be less 'play' and more learning.

As we become more aware of the implications of too early formal learning, the research of neuroscientists, educationalists, policy-makers and families may come to agree with the message 'too much too soon'. The programme and subsequent book based on Channel 4's 'Dispatches' programme (Mills 1998: 5) showed that compared with European settings, in the UK there is a difference in both approach and delivery of an early years curriculum. In UK settings, there is more emphasis on early reading and writing skills and less emphasis on music, movement and the oral linguistic approach.

All the teaching involves children having absolute confidence with manipulating concrete objects before moving on to representations of objects. However, Curtis (1994) observes that play in Eastern European nurseries described as 'imaginative and free-play' is what would be described in the UK as 'a drama lesson'. The debate comes full circle about interpretations and meanings, although it is widely accepted that play is the principal way in which children learn, the understanding and interpretation of play varies.

## Interpreting play ▋

Bruce (1991) describes what she calls 'free flow play' – what children do when they are given the freedom to follow their own ideas and interests, in their own way and for their own reasons, with appropriate or no adult involvement or direction. There is no previously identified end-product or rating scale to meet. Bruce describes play as coordinating a network of developmental and learning strategies, which have 12 features. When all or most of these features are present, it becomes 'free flow play'. Free flow play occurs, Bruce tells us, when children are able to use their experience of ideas, feelings, relationships and movement, and are able to apply them with control, competence and mastery. Bruce points out that all emotions – pride, anger, joy, a sense of loss and rejection – are found in free flow play. Children are helped to deal with grief, loss and anger through their free flow play. However Bruce (1991) also observes that 'many of the things called play by those of us working with children are not so' (p. 1).

The key contexts of play, which are physical, social and symbolic, help us to interpret children's actions and activities. Piaget (1962) saw play as the means by which the child's learning comes together and helps the child to make sense of the world. Vygotsky (1978) emphasized the importance of social interaction, of other people involved in play. He describes children's learning from a point he called the zone of proximal development to the zone of actual development).

## Play with people – play with objects

Much of child development theory, including the subject of play, is based on a European and North American perspective. Cole (1998) argues that children's culture has to be a fundamental ingredient in the major influences on child development. Cole also points out differences in babies' cognitive development because of their culture, which he identifies as a 'bio-social-behavioural shift', and the way in which babies interact with their environments. During tests, Japanese and American babies demonstrated the same behaviour towards objects. However, the American mothers behaved more positively towards their babies when the child was interested and playing with an object rather than themselves. They would divert the children's play away from themselves towards the object. The Japanese mothers behaved more positively when the baby showed more interest towards them in their play, rather than to an object.

In North American culture, typically it would appear that independence is seen to be more important than dependence (Cole 1998). However, as children mature, the differences in the play that they are best at correspond to the differences in their mothers' behaviour. The environment in which the child develops and grows needs to be a social one, including people, cultural beliefs, values and practices, supported by cultural tools and artefacts from the child's experiences and environment.

## Toys are not only appealing to babies

Trevarthen (1998) tells us that human life is essentially cooperative, sharing and exchanging ideas, interests, actions and play. Very young children learn about turn-taking through interpreting cues with a key adult (usually the mother), and playing conversational games, which is essential for later language development. These are the early games of babies, actions and interactions.

Stern (1991) observes that toys are not very appealing to babies; they prefer mobiles, which move like humans. It is the quality of the interactions, according to Bodrova and Long (1998), that affects the ability later to acquire mature levels of play. They suggest fewer 'toys' but more interactions with people. I agree that close interactions are crucial for developing play; these are the beginnings of complex social skills. However, the role of the adult is not to demonstrate the various ways for the young child to use the toys; think how frustrating this is for the baby or toddler who cannot yet manipulate the object in the same skilful way as the demonstrating adult. Babies need to be given time to explore, to manipulate objects and to interact with other babies and adults, the objects being precursors to pretend play. Then play will begin.

## Children with special educational needs and disabilities

Babies exploring their own bodies through their hands and feet can do so alone or as part of a game with an adult. Babies with specific needs may need adults to support these early explorations. Children with a visual impairment use their hands to be part of play experiences and fully participate. Children need to access all contexts of play: physical, social and symbolic. This can be challenging for practitioners working with children with specific needs. They need to be creative to encourage and support play in children whose perceptions and understanding of their surroundings are likely to be very different from adults'.

Jennings (2002) suggests that adults working with children with visual impairments should use the following strategies to be more effective in supporting these children's play:

- observing the child's signals;
- giving enriched descriptions;
- providing rich real experiences;
- giving choice and control;
- making sure the child is having fun on their terms.

Jennings' principles can be applied inclusively to all children's play.

## Adults helping children play alone

Adults sometimes finish something off for a baby, for example putting a stacking beaker on top of another, or picking up the baby, move them to another area of the nursery floor, without warning, saying: '... There, that's what you wanted isn't it?' and move off, leaving the baby bewildered, facing a new piece of equipment of the adult's choosing. We need to ask ourselves, what does this sort of action demonstrate about the child's rights? We need to think about what happens when a baby is trying to reach an object during that first journey towards movement, and watches as the unaware adult moves the toy or object a little further out of reach. The frustration of trying to play very often leads to the baby giving up. Babies can become withdrawn and unresponsive after attempts to play and communicate have been misunderstood or missed by adults, who are not attuned with the changing and developing needs of very young children.

This brings us to debate on the role of the adult in the support and development of young children's play. Early years practitioners cannot do this easily if they themselves have not experienced rich play or do not understand that babies need people, time and space.

Babies look for reactions and responses from everyone and everything around them. From those responses the beginning of emotional understanding begins. Stern (1991) called this attunement. However, if nursery practitioners are not tuned in to understand and respond to the signals babies use, then babies will be left to struggle, if there is too much struggle and not enough response from the adult, the baby then begins to withdraw, and may even appear 'self-contained'.

This kind of behaviour can have wide-reaching effects, as a study on older children demonstrated (Ball 1992). Goldschmied reminds us that adults often look at grizzling babies surrounded by toys and assume that their behaviour is for no good reason, as they have plenty of playthings. Goldschmied suggests that we should look at it from the babies' viewpoint.

> ...unlike adults, babies are dependent upon our imaginative understanding of what their needs are, and our willingness to provide *the means by which they can pursue their own learning for themselves*.
>
> (my emphasis) (Goldschmied 1989: 9)

First experiences for a baby are mostly inter-linked with adults – touching faces and fingers, and reaching for clothing and interesting accompaniments, as those of us who wear ear-rings, particularly the 'dangly' variety, will recognize, as these are grabbed or pulled as part of babies' play. These objects also serve to build up an image of 'who's who' for the baby. It is a shame that in many out-of-home care situations, practitioners who work with babies are required to wear protective overalls and are not able to wear jewellery (within reason) that is part of their personality or culture. Whilst understanding all the health and safety precautions necessary, it could be reasonable for practitioners to ensure that overalls are worn only for feeding and changing purposes. Uniform, although seen by many as helpful to ensure that staff are easily identifiable, means that babies and young children are often scanning a sea of same-colour T-shirts and have to find other identifiable signs to find their key person.

At only a few days old, babies are already organizing their images of the world, following moving objects with their eyes. Movement helps young children to understand where objects begin and end, rather than simply relying on edges to give information. Babies, as they play, are applying principles very early on in order to make sense of the world. Newborn babies will turn their heads and look towards an interesting noise, suggesting that they already expect to see something in the direction of the noise. Babies are able to imitate at only a few hours old, Meltzoff carried out research in a maternity hospital to prove that imitation was innate (reported in Gopnik, Meltzoff and Kuhl 1999: 30). The youngest baby he filmed was only 42 minutes old. The photograph opposite shows my colleague's husband and Niamh, aged 2 hours, imitating her proud new father.

## Science and babies

> A famous physicist was once asked, 'what is the use of pure science?', to which he replied, 'What is the use of a baby?' In other words, both are packed with potential for the future.
>
> (Goldschmied 1989: 1)

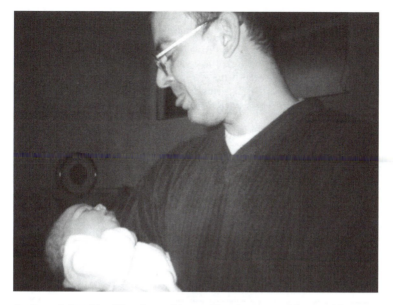

*Andy and daughter Niamh – poking out her tongue at 2 hours old.*

We have more evidence now from the neuroscientists which confirms what Goldschmied (1989) knew from her observations of babies at play, that they were far more knowing and knowledgeable than had been appreciated by the scientific community. The challenge as we discover even more about the workings of the brain is how we as educators (all adults involved with children are educators) use that knowledge.

Colin Blakemore (2000), talking about the results of recent brain research, gives a clear message about the relevance of this work for early years practitioners. He argues that people responsible for formulating a framework for very young children need to start thinking about the development of the brain, because those of us working with these young children, as carers and educators, can and do influence and shape brain development. Blakemore emphasizes the importance of social development and communication for young children, matching up with Vygotsky's theory of the social process of learning, with and through other people. He also confirms the intuitive thoughts and feelings of many practitioners and parents about the need to play.

One benefit of knowing the science is a kind of protective scepticism. It should make us deeply suspicious of any enterprise that offers a formula for making babies smarter or teaching them more from flash cards to Mozart tapes to Better Baby Institutes. Everything we know about these babies suggests that these artificial inventions are at best useless and at worst distractions from the normal interaction between grownups and babies.

(Gopnik, Meltzoff and Kuhl 1999: 201)

Babies need rich, real experiences. They need an 'abundance of experiences' (Thorp 2003) – experiences of real objects, real people and lots of conversation, not television programmes or videos. Communicating with babies about what they are experiencing is vital. Communicating through sign, facial expressions, body languages, are all part of this as adults observe and support babies and young children in their play.

## Play is vital

Practitioners working with or interested in children under 3 will need to consider that young children (especially those under 3) do not need 'activities' to draw round templates, focus on a colour of the week, or be part of themes or topics that have no relevance to their interests or understanding.

Blakemore explains that synapse formation seems to coincide with the emergence of various skills, hence the need to 'match the curriculum'. Early experiences and play have a direct impact on the brain-wiring process. At 3 months the visual cortex peaks, fine-tuning the connections which enable the eyes to focus. By 6 months of age, synapses form at such a rate that the brain consumes far more energy than an adult brain, and synapse formation continues for up to 10 years.

By the time children reach 2 years of age, they have approximately the same number of synapses as an adult, which is 50 per cent less than the baby was born with. The message from Blakemore was 'use it, don't lose it'.

The research shows us that baby's brains are at their most plastic (flexible), rapidly moulding and fitting into its surroundings. The potential for development is staggering. It seems that there are sensitive periods, when early learning must meet and match the developing brain. The treasure basket is one opportunity for young babies to play and be 'in charge of their own learning', as we will explore later on in the book.

## Play, growth and development

Everything we do with a child has some potential physical influence on the rapidly growing brain. This has implications for the way in which we plan for very young children's play and learning, whether in a large or small out-of-home setting. The way in which we learn about and respond to babies' play and communication signals is vital for their emotional wellbeing, which in turn affects the future development of play and learning. An emotionally secure child, equipped with a high level of social skills, able to read and respond to others' signals is more likely to learn effectively. (Manning-Morton and Thorp 2003). Those key adults parents and carers, through their responses and reactions, will have laid the foundations of emotional literacy, because it seems that it is affective early experiences that are key to all learning.

During a series of observations of a group of babies who had played regularly together at the treasure basket as part of a small research project, I watched as Harry, aged 10 months, and Alice, aged 7 months, were seated at the basket with Sarah, Alice's key person, seated close by.

Harry watches Alice playing with the linked spoons. He is distracted by her short cry, Alice is reassured again by Sarah (the adult), through some gentle stroking of Alice's back. Alice leans into the basket and strokes the shoe brush, cries and turns away. Alice is distracted by the whistling of the window cleaner, Harry looks at Alice and then follows her gaze to the window. Harry strokes the large shell positioned in between his legs. He then continues to gently rummage in the basket. He has moved slightly away from the side of the basket and is sitting/leaning precariously. Harry's mother arrives and in his delight at her voice, he completely overbalances. She picks him up. Harry quickly stops crying and smiles broadly.

## An unsettled baby cannot play

Alice was still unsettled at the basket during this time, she needed and received reassurance from Sarah, and was still only exploring objects fleetingly. She was easily distracted and at times distracted Harry. There was definite interaction between the two babies and Harry appears, not for the first time during my observations, to show concern for Alice's distress. Sarah tuned in to Alice's needs. She had been offering Alice verbal reassurance, 'it's okay Alice, Sarah is here, everything is okay', and keeping close eye contact with her, responding with reassuring glances and smiles to Alice. At my suggestion Sarah slid her arm across, and stroked Alice's back. This had an immediate effect, soothing Alice.

I had wanted to see if Alice needed more than the reassuring glances that Goldschmied suggests. I did not want to take Alice away from the basket, but to support her with her struggles. During discussions, the practitioner reported that they 'seemed to pick her up a lot'. As Alice is still settling into the nursery, getting to know Sarah and the team, it is a difficult time for her. She needs reassurance and to know that she will be supported through cuddles and lots of talk. However, being picked up by three different members of the team during the day may not be helping her to resettle and develop her play. An unsettled child cannot play. The practitioner team agreed to be consistent with Alice, not to immediately pick her up if she cried, but to sit close to her and talk with her, touch her, and carry on playing together. Sarah, as the key person, was to be the main source of support for Alice as she settled into the nursery.

The length of time needed for babies to develop close relationships and become comfortable in a new setting so that their play develops varies. There are no set rules and every baby will be different and have different needs. It is important for each setting to draw up its own plans for settling in new families, ensuring that the emotional needs of parents are recognized and responded to. Then parents will see them settle and be able to leave their babies, seeing them beginning to play. The settling in process for parents needs to be planned for as carefully as the welcoming and settling of a new baby. Parents and carers may need support in how to be the emotional anchors for very young babies, and it is crucial that all settings draw up a plan to help all those working with children under 3, where the role and relationship of a key person and secure attachments are responded to and recognized.

If play is to develop and contribute to the child's wellbeing, then it must be anchored in secure emotional and social development. Supportive, supporting and responsive adults are the anchors in these aspects of development, knowing when to hold fast or raise the anchor.

## Key points from this chapter

- All the adults in an early years setting, need secure emotional anchors;
- Babies need to develop close attachments with key adults outside the home who share in their care, play and learning, in order to begin to play;
- Practitioners need to debate and discuss the range of information and materials available for babies and young children, ensuring it focuses on the characteristics and interests of the child, not on developmental stages or inappropriate curriculum guidance;
- Babies and young children need rich and real experiencess;
- An unsettled baby cannot play.

# 2

# EARLY PLAY AND PLAYTHINGS – CROSSING CULTURES

The earliest human societies had few toys to offer their children and even fewer for under-ones to play with. The !Kung San infant in Africa's Kalahari Desert plays with his mother's person, her beads, her hair. Later he will graduate to make 'toys' from twigs and flowers, insects and stones. His imagination must work overtime to create his own, unique fantasy world.

(Jackson 2002: 25)

Babies' and young children's needs have not really changed. They need people who enjoy their company, find their play and attempts at conversation interesting and inspiring enough to respond to and

*Special adults, special play moments, no other playthings necessary.*

develop. The plethora of toys and 'must haves' for babies and young children to 'play with' has grown over history, and modern babies and young children appear, if baby catalogues and manuals are anything to go by, to 'need' a vast amount.

Babies communicate with adults and other babies not only through non-verbal signals and orally, but through objects. This has been well documented by observers of very young children such as Goldschmied and Selleck (1996). This is the beginning of babies' play, as they look for a response or are in the position of offering a response, which results in another response, a reciprocal relationship of perhaps eyebrows raising, mouths opening, or objects being offered. 'Have a look at this, what do you think, tell me about it, talk to me, make that funny face again, sing that song ...' Play in every culture reflects the experience of babies and children.

## Early play: What do babies begin to play with and how? ▮

Parents the world over would probably answer in the same way. They will have watched their very young babies finding and then playing with their feet, fists, fingers, bits of cot blanket or sheet, playing with the breeze as it blows curtains or mosquito nets, babbling and chattering to the mobile or the toy in the cot, or perhaps like the !Kung San babies playing with an adult's face, hair, pulling at noses, finding out where this new play object begins and ends. Babies are born problem-solvers; they want to know what things are and what they do; at just a few days old they turn away from objects looming towards them, aware that there is physicality to an object, or turn their head away from a bright light, or track a slow-moving object with head and eye movements (Murray and Andrews 2000). We can already begin to see that the baby who is beginning to play is seeking answers to as yet unasked questions, and testing objects and people for responses.

At only a few days old babies gaze, cross-eyed but intently, at striped objects or complex patterns of high contrast. Many commercial playthings appearing on the Western market for babies feature black, white and red patterns of stripes, checks and bulls eyes. Mobiles, borders of mirrors, soft blocks and rattles are produced using these colours to encourage play and learning. An upsurge in attention to developmental psychologists' tests on babies has resulted in the manufacture of these types of playthings, labelled and sold as 'educational', to give baby a 'good start'. Naturally, babies prefer these colours and patterns so will spend longer staring and following the mobiles or toys. Babies like stripes because of the sharp contrast between the brightness and the texture of two surfaces. They pay attention to the edges of the images and are able to work out the beginning and the end of the object.

## Pleasing babies for play times

It becomes more crucial that adults charged with looking after other people's babies take the time and space to observe carefully. Babies rely on the adults around them to respond and meet their ever-changing needs. What is the right response one day may need to be changed the next.

When setting out the baby-space in a group setting, it is vital to look at where you are going to place babies, from the babies' per-spective. Will the sun be in their eyes, is the light on the mirror too reflective, and is there a draught or unattractive sounds? Imagine sitting in a baby bouncer or lying on the nursery floor every day next to a wall where the nappy dispenser reverberates in your ears continually or a door is continually opened and closed, and not being able to move away independently! These are important and need to be thought about in the planning and designing stage of a setting.

However, there are other things that practitioners must think about in terms of the babies' play, comfort and interests, such as learning to read babies' expressions and movements, recognizing and responding to distress. Having a plan for settling in families and very young babies is so important, as discussed in the previous chapter. Practitioners will need to spend time with the parents and carers to begin to learn about the baby's signals and expressions in order to support learning through play. Practitioners working with children under 3, and particularly those with very young babies under 1 year, will need support (see Goldschmied 1994), high ratios of caregivers to children is essential, as is continuity of care, consistent care, high-quality care.

Play as currently understood is a relatively late phenomenon in the history of child development. Play is a complex process to study and, as Bruce (1997) reminds us, we are still gathering natural history data. However, in England there has been an inclination by some practitioners working with children younger than 3 years old to work towards and be focused on the curricula of children 3 years and older. This has often meant children as young as 2 being expected to sit and complete worksheets of 'colours and numbers', or trace pre-printed pictures to develop their 'pencil control', or to be involved in themes or topics of which they have little or no understanding or experience – pirates, jungles, space, and a whole raft of other inappropriate practices. Particularly when planning for children under 3, the child's interests should lead the activity or experience. By identifying what these children are interested in and what they like to spend time doing and watching, practitioners are then able to plan for children's individual and relevant interests.

## Treasure baskets as artefacts of the child's culture

Elinor Goldschmied (1989) conceived the idea of the treasure basket. Using her many observations whilst working with babies in full-time care environments in Italy and the UK she observed that: 'Babies used their five senses along with their co-ordination of eye and hand in playing with objects, which in their various ways offer them a rich stimulus.' Treasure baskets are explored and played with in depth in Chapter 6.

A treasure basket can become an artefact of culture, and cross cultural boundaries to enhance the context and content of a child's culture. A well-stocked basket with carefully selected objects can give babies the opportunities to explore those things that make up their world. Human life experiences can begin as babies around the basket:

- play alone;
- play cooperatively;
- share interest in objects and each other.

Many children in the Western world, and in the UK today, are protected from playing with everyday things. The fear of becoming dirty or of children hurting themselves is very real, and from a very early age many children are introduced to sterile imitations of their world. In the home and in many other settings, plastic dominates play.

## Shake, rattle and roll

Goldschmied (personal communication 2003) described a dried gourd in her treasure basket, as 'the oldest rattle in the world'. Barnes (1998: 8), also talking about rattles, identifies gourds and turtle shells being used to make rattles for the children of Native Americans. She goes on to describe the clay rattles of the Egyptians and those made from hollow bamboo tubes and decorated with paper or silver in

Japan and China. Silver rattles made in Europe during the sixteenth and seventeenth centuries were engraved and decorated with coral.

## Doll play

The Museum of Childhood in Bethnal Green has the largest collection of children's playthings in England. Brooks (2000) writes about collections of dolls, dating from 1800–1960, displayed in various National Trust properties. An exhibition of dolls and toys I visited in Denmark includes a doll from 1690. Information by Stadelhofer and Johansen (2000) describe dolls in the exhibition and give a brief history. Just looking at the collection of dolls from around the world, it is clear that most dolls were never intended to be playthings, the detail of costume, intricacy of fastenings, mechanical heads, some made with blocks of wood for the bodies, bisque and porcelain heads. They were dressed with the clothes of the period, representing women, not men or children, and were often given as presents not for children, but for women.

Baby dolls did not appear until the beginning of the twentieth century. These started to look more like a baby, not a woman in baby's clothes. Even when they were eventually passed down to children to play with, it's hard to imagine them being played with.

Dolls are known from all civilizations. Barnes describes dolls made of earthenware found in Greece and of miniature pots excavated from tombs and archaeological sites.

As we observe children today in the role-play area setting out tables for cafés and playing out the rituals of their families' and culture's mealtimes, we can imagine small children since early times, playing 'home' all over the world with objects from their culture and environment.

Tea sets and cooking implements are still an important resource in an early years setting, for young children real-sized cups, pots and plates are far better than the plastic imitations. During the eighteenth century tea-sets were manufactured in Europe; these were often highly decorated and made from fine porcelain, almost too precious for playing with. Entire dinner services were made and small girls were encouraged to practise the expected roles of hostess, homemaker and cook (Barnes 1998: 6).

## Baby art

Period paintings show us a little of what life was like for young babies and children. 'Babies in Art' (1997) has pictures of babies taken from famous paintings around the world; these include the painting 'Master Baby' by Sir William Quiller Orchardson (1832–1910), hanging in the Edinburgh National Gallery, which shows a very young baby lying on a drawing room sofa looking up at a fan being waved by a smiling female, possibly his adoring mother. The close-up of the baby's face shows us clearly how the painter has captured the intentness of the baby's gaze. If you watch babies gazing at objects being waved above them, you will often see their fingers curl and uncurl as in the painting. One can imagine the joyful squeals as his fingers curl and uncurl in delight as his mother's hand waves and flaps the fan to keep his attention whilst they sat for the painter.

Perhaps she is singing to him and he is 'conducting', an idea described by Trevarthen (2000) to which we will return later in the book. Another of my favourite pictures is *Gabrielle with Jean*, by Pierre-Auguste Renoir (1841–1919). This shows a young child and a woman engrossed in playing together with either sand or a very early version of 'gloop' (cornflour and water). It is not easy to define the substance, but it is clearly a very early messy play activity! Here, the painter has captured the child's complete attention on the activity. Both woman and child are so close together, and a sense of oneness and absolute security in the activity comes across from the painting.

## Manufactured play

Many resources available today for babies are labelled 'educational' by the manufacturers, and those concerned with developing fine manipulative skills or memory usually have a pre-determined result, a right or wrong way to use them. Few, if any, of these toys, the majority of which are made of plastic, encourage or allow babies to pursue their own learning. The square brick from the shape sorter will only go into the square hole. What else is there for the baby to explore?

The brick is plastic. The surface is smooth and slippery. It is not easy to maintain a grasp with fingers that have become moist from the motion of going between mouth and the brick itself being mouthed. The container for the bricks may provide some short-term interest in that it can be banged or patted or mouthed. Usually, though, this sort of exploration is interrupted by an adult demonstrating where the square brick should really go: 'Look, it goes in the box, the square hole, lets drop it in shall we?' and they promptly do it for the watching baby. Babies should occasionally have these demonstrations, but I disagree with Bodrova and Long (1998: 280) when they suggest that the role of the adult is 'to demonstrate various ways to use these toys'. The 'what' and 'how to' approach to 'do things properly' (from an adult's perspective) often means no time for the baby to play and lack of opportunity for the exploratory process.

## Key points from this chapter

- Play in every culture reflects the experience of babies and young children;
- People are important playthings;
- Playthings do not have to cost the earth or be a cost to the earth environmentally;
- Play and playthings in early years settings should reflect and value the culture of very young babies and children.

# 3

# 'AND ME': PLAY WITH SIGNIFICANT OTHERS

'Our families are where we first learn about ourselves.'
(Bradshaw, quoted in Miles 1994: 194)

We have begun to think about the adult in relation to babies' play. This chapter now focuses on the importance of significant others. People outside of the immediate family who play a part in caring for and educating children have a significant effect on the development of the young child's play and learning.

## Parents

Talking with a group of parents, I asked them what had made them choose a particular nursery for their babies. They were all first-time parents, returning to some kind of paid employment, and sharing the care of their baby with a partner. Some parents had made a pre-arranged visit to an early years setting and had arrived to find the staff who worked with the babies had gone out for a walk – so they had no opportunity to talk to the people who might be looking after their baby or watch other babies and the practitioners playing together. The settling-in period and how the nursery welcomed families into the new environment was also crucial to parents final decision.

Meeting and settling in are part of normal routines and good practice for early years settings. They are also crucial to the beginnings of babies' play. Babies and families need to feel settled and that the practitioners are interested in knowing about and finding out about their developing and changing needs. Then they can begin forming secure relationships with practitioners. It is the beginning of making connections. What is this baby or young child interested in? What can I do, and how do I begin the building of this relationship?

'*And me*' is not just about babies relationships with early years practitioners, it is about the relationship practitioners need to develop with parents and families. Goldschmied and Selleck (1996: 12) talk of the 'triangle of trust and communication' needed between the parent, practitioner and baby. I think this is crucial before any play can begin. Staff need to feel comfortable about the intimacy of their relationship with parents and carers, for they will be playing intimate games with their babies and sharing special moments. It is about practitioners understanding and explaining the relationship they will develop with the baby or young child as one of affection not possession.

A training session on the role of the key person, for practitioners from a variety of settings, focused on and explored their understanding of the key person approach, how different settings worked the approach, how to introduce it, and the benefits and challenges of the approach. During the day, a practitioner from a full-day care setting shared her experience of the beginning of a relationship with a new child and family. After a period of time, the child's parent confided to her, 'I hate it if he cries when we come to nursery and I have to leave him. I hate it when he runs to you.'

In early years settings the staff teams will need opportunities to discuss some of the difficult and sometimes painful issues around looking after other people's babies and young children. Playing and spending time with other people's very young children can raise all sorts of issues around jealousy, guilt and inadequacy for some families. Sharing information about intimate and special times has to be done sensitively. Some parents will want to know whether the baby has almost tottered their first step alone, so that they can be sure not to miss or to encourage the next attempt. For some parents this will be a no-go area, and it is crucial to know what the parent will want to hear and how. A Polaroid taken in the nursery of the first time the child stands or those first steps may be a treasured possession or it may be too painful, a reminder of the things that the parent is missing.

The settling-in time when the practitioner and the parent begin to get to know each other is also a time for the parent to come into the nursery and join in the routines, introducing the baby or young child to the spaces where he or she will play and to the places where he or she will sleep, be changed and be fed. Everything is changing for the young baby or child when other people become part of their care and play, so practitioners will need to consider keeping the routines and patterns of feeding and sleeping as familiar as possible.

Work documented at Pen Green Children's Centre (in Whalley 2001) shows that when parents are involved in their children's play and learning, the experience will be a richer and more positive experience for the child. It becomes even more essential that early years practitioners involved in the care, play and learning of very young children, in an out-of-home setting, examine their own settings' principles for working with parents and caring for very young children. Every member of the practitioner team expected to deliver the principles should be involved in the decisions about those principles.

Bruce (1987, 1997) talked about 'the child in the family/community', where the three strands of the early childhood curriculum, 'child, curriculum, context', are balanced, the family experiences and parents' knowledge being that vital 'context' of the child. Early years practitioners must ensure that the parent's contribution to their child's early learning experiences is valued and encouraged. Parents are the first and most significant figures for the child. The early years practitioner will become another important figure. Ball (1992: 48) concludes that 'Children are more likely to thrive (and learn) in a secure triangle of care provided by parents, professionals and the community as a whole'. If we add 'play' then this statement sums everything up.

## Parents talking ... ■

Talking with parents is crucial, whether it be at the front door of the setting, on the telephone, informally or formally, about the countless issues and ideas to do with the play, care and learning of their baby or young child. This will be something all practitioners and managers of early years settings are familiar with. When I talked to one group of parents about their reasons for choosing day care (Forbes 1993), 65 per cent of them told me that they had chosen their current nursery on the recommendation of another parent. A further group of parents in 1999 reiterated this.

### *Making choices*

Some parents might be unaware of the importance and link between close attachments and play; they might choose a nursery or group setting as a place where they think that their child will not have to get too close to another person. For some, the possibility of a close relationship between a childminder and a young child is a threat, and for others the one-to-one relationship is crucial. Parents need to be offered choices and given explanations as to how a group setting caring for very young babies and children organizes and delivers their provision to ensure that close, secure emotional relationships form between the child and the practitioner and how parents are included and valued in the setting.

Even without a key person approach, it is important that practitioners working with babies and young children have stable and constant relationships. In some settings practitioners are assigned to be with a baby over a given period of time. Assigning a small number of children to a particular group is essential (Elfer 2000), so that opportunities for one-to-one time can be planned in and experiences such as 'island of intimacy', as described by Goldschmied and Jackson (1994: 41), can be considered by practitioners and used in a way that works for the diversity of each setting. These 'island times', as I now refer to them, are special moments when the key person and their familiar group have time together to share news and new objects, which Goldschmied identified as an especially useful opportunity for encouraging, listening to and assessing individual children's language development (1994: 135). Think of them as very intimate circle times for children up to 3 years, when not having to sit and wait for too long for 'my turn' is crucial, creating safe, familiar time slots during the day when the key person is completely focused on their own small group of children and is not responsible for other routines of the setting, or other children.

I have found during training sessions practitioners who are unsure of the key person approach, but on further discussion they have often discovered that they are implementing some of the essential aspects of the approach, and further debate has then supported the development of practice for the setting and their colleagues.

Parents need to know how and why play is so crucial to a baby's development and how the setting or person caring for that child will ensure that the baby has lots of opportunities for play.

## Asking parents and families about choosing childcare

Cryer and Burchinal (1997: 35), in a research study on 'Parents as Childcare Consumers', state '. . . that the concept of parents as consumers who can make informed choices about childcare is controversial'. This was a study of 727 parents of children under 3 and

2407 parents of pre-schoolers. Certain aspects of the day care provision were identified as easier to observe and quality rate, however the study suggested that parents appeared unlikely to match the childcare they purchased for their young children to their childcare values. The study also suggested that 'imperfect information could hinder parents from demanding the aspects of high-quality childcare which they believe to be important for their children' (1997: 53).

Parents as active 'consumers' has become a buzz word, however the emphasis has to be on developing an inclusive environment where the parent becomes an active partner. In order for parents to really be active partners they need to know about the things that matter in early years out-of-home settings. Play matters and we need to include information about the importance of young children's play and learning in any information parents are given about the setting. If settings are to work in a spirit of cooperation and partnership with parents, as the *National Standards* (2001) and the *English Birth to Three Matters Framework* (2002) suggest, then practitioners need to value the play and learning that happens at home, before the baby or young child join an early years setting and implement and maintain effective communication with parents about their children's developing play patterns and behaviour.

## Using play language

We need to use language that is accessible to all the families using early years provision, and use specific languages for the individual early years setting and community. Language describing young children's play needs to be acknowledged and shared. Practitioners can begin to do this through discussions and written observations, photographs shared can help to describe a specific moment or example and can help parents describe play behaviour seen at home or elsewhere. Notice boards, information about policies and procedures, and newsletters and reports could be shared in a range of media to include words, pictures and photographs.

A shared language in an early years setting is essential. A shared language and understanding of babies and young children beginning to play is crucial.

## Real partnerships

> A conceptual gulf exists between parents and professionals
> on such issues as play, creativity, messing about with raw
> materials, individuality, self-regulation, reading readiness and
> so on
>
> (Athey 1990: 60)

Athey describes how parents viewed and treated the professionals from the Froebel Project with 'reverence'. It was only after a period of working together, working things out together, and agreeing to accommodate each others' views and attitudes that agreement was reached on how to help individual children. Parents were genuinely respected and recognized as experts on their own children. Home books were used, as were practitioners' and parents' recorded observations and information. Parents were part of their children's play, involved in the learning about their children and in a wider educational context.

Inviting and creating an environment of parental partnership may bridge the gulf of 'reverence'. Parents need to know that rich play experiences and opportunities are essential to what makes a childcare setting a quality setting. Then parents can begin to make choices and be part of the quality development of play.

A framework of agreed and understood principles is a starting point. If a setting does not have these agreements about ethos and practice, then there will be little opportunity for play to flourish and develop. There will be little opportunity for the development of deeper play for the babies and young children or for the practitioners to explore and debate the play behaviour. There needs to be a common understanding of the language used and expectations of delivery.

The principles that underpin the *English Birth to Three Matters Framework (2002: 4)* include those linked to babies and young children's play and learning experiences, where learning is seen as a shared process and a relationship with a key person at home and in the setting is essential to young children's wellbeing. If a setting takes these principles on board, all the practitioners will need to work through them in order to put them into practice. Sharing principles with parents and families is vital in ensuring the families who use the settings are receiving the play, care and learning experiences that their children are entitled to. For some practitioners, thinking that they are more important than the resources and equipment will be a challenge. How many managers of early years settings have heard the constant plea for more resources? We need to be able to see and feel the play and learning that goes on in a setting, and so should parents. Understanding that adults who care for and support children's play are more important than an early years setting crammed full of expensive playthings and resources can be a difficult concept for some practitioners and parents.

## Welcomes: getting to know the early years setting

### *Making connections*

Parents need to get to know their way round the early years setting, the layout of the building, how outside spaces are used, and find out about policies and procedures and how the early years setting works. Documentation particular to the setting and that required by, in England, Ofsted and the local Early Years Childcare and Development Partnership, will need completing.

Parents are the most important people in their children's lives. It is from parents that children learn most, particularly in the early months and years. The critical input of the parents in the child's development and early learning is self-evident – and yet frequently ignored 'the closer the links between parent and nursery . . . the more effective that learning becomes' (Ball 1992: 43).

All the staff in the setting and the practitioners need to know about the child's current interests – what they like to do, how they do it. Likes, dislikes, interests, sleep patterns, allergies, medical information, eating habits and food preferences of the child are all vital. Families are usually encouraged to share as much information as they can with a key person. This person is likely to become a 'significant adult' in the family's life. Finding out about what the baby or young child is interested in, likes to do, how they like to be held, handled, cuddled, what makes the baby laugh, what games they are familiar with, songs to be sung, are all part of beginning to play with a new person.

### *Settling in . . . ready to play*

Settling-in visits, when the baby or young child gradually spends longer and longer at the early years setting, need to be arranged around the parents as well as the practical constraints of the setting. Time needs to be allocated to enable the identified key person to be away from the other children to spend time with the parent. The parent needs to complete the setting documents and this must be done sensitively. For some this could be an exposure of the limitations of their own literacy skills and, although most early years settings have a deluge of paper to be completed, each setting must ensure parents are supported in the completion of vital information. It might mean the key person doing lots of talking, asking questions and recording the parents' responses, then checking the information back with the parent – a conversation might go like this.

---

### Checking back conversation

... so Hannah is really interested in playing with bags at the moment, you have noticed how she likes to put things inside them and carry them around with her. That's great, we can see what she does here, and we have lots of handbags, shopping bags. We'll watch her play here for a week and then talk again about what we think she is trying to find out.

---

This settling in time, and it may well be over several weeks, with the key person, should include talking about the baby, parent, extended family, anything the parent feels is helpful and anything not offered that the practitioner feels is essential being skilfully and sensitively raised. It is the beginning of the 'getting to know you both' process. This is important to enable a baby to feel secure enough to begin playing and exploring, finding out about his or her new environment; these new faces and smells will only be played with if the baby is feeling emotionally secure.

## Practitioners talking...

Managers and practitioners from early years settings found that parents who spent time with their babies and young children during this settling-in period, taking part in the daily care routines and playing with them, helped the children to settle. Being in the setting, joining in with activities and key events, for example settling the baby to sleep in a different cot, with sheets that do not smell of 'my home', was reassuring and helpful to the baby. This is the beginning of a trusting relationship between the key person, parent and baby, where through exploring and playing the message from parent to baby was 'this is okay, because I wouldn't be here playing with you and supporting you if it wasn't'.

Each early years setting will have a different approach to partnership with parents, and many settings encourage parents to become involved in a variety of ways. However, parents need to know that early years practitioners are not competing for the baby's or young child's affection. The parent–child attachment is crucial, and the relationship between baby and practitioner is quite different; it is about affection not possession.

Respect for parents and how that is demonstrated in the early years setting is also critical – how are families spoken to, what are the 'hidden' messages on notice boards, in reports or daily notes home, saying to parents? Practitioners need to reflect on their practice and conversations to ensure that families are not being undermined or made to feel less competent in their parenting knowledge and skills. It is a fine line and one that practitioners need to contemplate and debate.

Practitioners also need to acknowledge that all families are different and there will be those who want to share everything about their family history and current events on a daily basis, and those who want to keep a more distant relationship with the practitioners and the setting. Experienced practitioners can support colleagues in ensuring that families are treated as individuals, and that those parents who are less confident about taking part in the life of the setting can be encouraged to play as much or as little as is right for them.

### Following up new families and young children: How are you?

It is important to check out how new families and young children are settling into the early years setting. Carrying out an informal review meeting with the parent is one way. This gives the practitioner the opportunity to ensure that any queries to do with policies and procedures can be discussed, but also review the first six to eight weeks from the young child's perspective. This time frame allows for parents, children and practitioners to have accumulated experiences, opinions and questions. The questions that might be useful could include:

• How have things been for the family, what about at home?
• Are routines different or difficult?
• What about the baby's or young child's play, how is it developing or changing?

Building those early bridges, as Goldschmied (1994) describes the process of getting to know parents, encouraging the flow of information between nursery and home, will help to allay some anxieties and enable parents to develop strong relationships with the key workers. This is a useful time to revisit earlier discussions and information about the setting. Then the play can begin! Parents and practitioners can begin the discussions about play and how opportunities in daily routines offer babies and young children perfect experiences for play.

## Communicating – sharing play experiences

For parents and practitioners, how they communicate about the young child's experiences whilst in an out-of-home setting is crucial. Early years settings may use a range of methods, daily report sheets, diaries, weekly reports, notice boards and of course talking to each other. The conversations between parent and practitioner at the beginning and end of the day are crucial, and sensitive practitioners are acutely aware of what to listen for and what to ask. Whilst recording and sharing all the information regarding a baby's or very young child's care needs is vital, so too is sharing the play experiences and opportunities.

Parents can be encouraged to share with the setting their own observations of the baby's play. A dialogue can be built up to inform the planning for play in the setting and support parents' understanding of their child's play and learning. When parents are able to spend time in the setting it is essential to be flexible and try hard not to say 'this is not a good time'! It might not be the very best day/time for you, but it could be the only day for the parent, and you can be sure it will be the best day for that child with a family member in the setting. For some parents, being with a group of children, not just their own, may be daunting and if a parent has volunteered to take part or share a special skill, or simply wants to be part of their child's day, then settings need to learn to say 'yes' – every time. It is very easy to make assumptions and be judgemental, especially of working parents, that they will not be able to spend time in the setting and for practitioners to think about parents as 'they'. Greenman and Stonehouse (1997: 245) urge us to resist falling into this trap and not think of parents as 'a mutant species'. In this specimen group are '... the always late (rude and uncaring), the one who forgets things (irresponsible) ...'. They counter (1997: 245) this with the observation that although this may be the discussion of the staff room, those same practitioners usually have 'a bark that is worse than their bite and actually behave more sensitively and are more accommodating when interacting with parents'.

Watching parents and children arriving and leaving early years settings we will see many families who have made complex arrangements, enabling them to spend time finding out about their child's play and perhaps to join in for part of a day. Families need to be encouraged to share skills and experiences – as a real postal worker, a tap dancer, or a parent sharing experiences of food from another culture or bringing in a new brother or sister for these very young children to meet.

Parents need to be seen by practitioners as having different but equal strengths. This is one of the characteristics attributed to parents as partners in, rather than consumers of, services, described by Rodd (1998) on Wolfendale's work with parents. They need to be central in decision-making about their babies' and young children's play, care and learning. Home routines for babies need to be followed as closely as possible and routines are about the individual child. The *English Birth to Three Matters Framework (2000: 4)* suggests that 'schedules and routines flow with the child's needs'.

If the mutual respect is in place that enables the key worker to confidently share his or her experiences of the baby's day, the delights and discoveries, the parents will delight in that information. Most parents want to know, hear about and talk about their baby's or young child's play and learning experiences.

## Key points from this chapter

- Babies and families need healthy emotional attachments with the familiar, trusting, and secure relationship of a key person in order for play to develop;
- Babies need interested, interesting, excited practitioners – adults who think babies have a natural 'wow' factor as they begin to play;
- Practitioners need to be interested in, excited about, knowing and finding out about the baby's or young child's developing and changing play needs and experiences – boring or bored adults need not apply to work with babies and very young children!
- Practitioners need to begin making connections – what is this baby or young child interested in, what can I do and how can I begin the building of this relationship?
- Parents need opportunities to begin forming secure relationships with practitioners;
- Attachment relationships are about affection not possessiveness;
- Is day-to-day contact with families appropriate for all the diverse needs of adults and children in the setting?;
- How parents are informed about the play development of their children is important;
- How parents contribute about and to their children's play and learning experiences at home matters;
- How parents contribute about and to their children's play and learning experiences in the setting matters.

# 4

# BEGINNING TO MOVE

Movement is one of the ways in which very young babies make their needs and feelings known – the thrust of a limb, screwing up of the face, turning their face away, saying to the adult 'I have had enough of playing now thank you, leave me be for a while'. Movement is vital to babies' and young children's understanding of their actions and the effect they can have on other objects or people. Very young babies play, explore and express themselves through movement, some of which is so minute that parents and practitioners caring for other people's babies have to be good observers and interpreters.

Feelings, the level of involvement, whether a child is really interested in what is happening around them or in a particular play situation can be interpreted through movement and posture. This is why it is so important for practitioners caring for other people's babies to become attuned to babies' movements and feelings and be able to interpret and respond to them.

Movement starts before birth. Babies spend a lot of time moving about in utero, and those flutters of movement can be detected from about 17 weeks' gestation. How many siblings have been introduced to the expected baby through listening to the heartbeat or 'feeling the baby moving in Mummy's tummy'?

Bruce and Meggitt (2002) tell us that babies and young children link moving and learning through the senses. This is known as kinaesthesia. The sense of movement of our body is fundamental in the development of self.

For many childcare students, the way of learning about and thinking of children's movement will have been through their studies of physical development, looking at milestones or stages of development and thinking about movement as an aspect of the physical. However, although normative scales of development are useful to help us understand the predictable order that physical development takes, we should take heed of Goldschmied's story in the introduction to this book and remember that a hip is part of a person.

The *English Birth to Three Matters Framework* (2002) offers practitioners the holistic route; it has identified four 'aspects', to help us focus on the child:

A Strong Child                    A Skilful Communicator
A Competent Learner               A Healthy Child

These aspects celebrate the skill and competence of babies and young children. We can explore babies' play through movement within all these aspects, through growing and developing, making connections, being creative, being imaginative, representing, being together, and me, myself and I, all of which are components of the framework.

We can also think about movement in the context of babies' communication and play, perhaps as an early signalling device, which we need to decipher and respond to. Carter (1999: 85) tells us that young children respond to human faces from birth and that this skill improves all the time.

Murray and Andrews (2000: 19) tell us that a baby will respond to the sound of a human voice in preference to a similar-pitched sound and that this is based on his or her previous experiences. A baby will have heard and become familiar with the voices of those close to him or her. However, the response to voice sounds so soon after birth is also about preferring faces to inanimate objects.

In order to survive, babies come equipped to signal their needs and wants by movement and sound. Perhaps for many adults, identifying and responding to the sounds that we can hear is easier than to those we have to observe carefully to notice. One signal that we are most familiar with is when baby is telling us he has had enough, by yawning or frowning or we can see the baby turn his head away, tiring, after a period of play and conversation. Babies as young as 2.5 weeks have been recorded demonstrating this (Murray and Andrews 2000: 56). It is how we as adults respond to and respect the baby's request for some peace and quiet which is important!

In group settings it is even more important that the baby has a known adult or key person whom they can rely on to respond to their needs. Sensitive communication with families is essential to find out what the baby's personal signals are and how these are responded to. This will become part of an ongoing dialogue between family and out-of-home setting to ensure that the changing and developing signals are identified and interpreted together. Practitioners and parents need to be aware of those 'sensitive times' (Bruce and Meggitt 2002: 71) or periods of development when the area of the brain concerned with emotion is developing. Many practitioners will recognize the period when babies become more anxious about strangers and being left, around 8 months. Davies (2003) advises us to be aware that anxiety may not simply relate to the unfamiliar face, but also to an unfamiliar expression on a familiar face.

---

### Grandma's new glasses

We were visiting Grandma after a gap of several weeks, Alistair was around 9 months old, and he pulled several funny faces from the safety of my arms as Grandma greeted us on the doorstep, however she was quick to observe,

'Oh Alistair, don't you like my new glasses, I didn't think they were that different, I know it is a little while since you have seen me, come and talk to me in the kitchen whilst I make mummy and me a coffee.'

So whilst some familiar domestic tasks were carried out in an unfamiliar environment, Alistair was re-acquainted with Grandma (still from the safety of my arms) until he was ready to go to her for a 'proper cuddle and greeting'!

(I hadn't even noticed my Mother's new frames...)

---

Davies (2003: 32) advises that there is a parallel to be drawn with individuals being recognised through '...the tone, volume, and rhythmicality of the spoken word'. She goes on to suggest that this can help us to think about why conversely when a stranger offers familiar visual or sound patterns babies can become upset or 'disease'.

Babies cannot begin to play when they are unsure of the people around them, even though the environment may be familiar, the routine feeding times kept and familiar equipment used. The analogy for us could be when we go to see our doctor, we have psyched ourselves up for a check-up or discussion of something quite personal, when we are called in to the consulting room and it is not our own doctor. Does it matter? – the person is a doctor, has our notes, knows all about us, can probably answer our queries and concerns, can look after us – but it is not quite the same as having that contact with someone with whom we have already developed a relationship of trust. Practitioners need to think about this when planning staffing patterns and covering for absences in out-of-home settings with very young children, recognizing that babies need to be introduced to new faces amongst the security of those familiar carers.

## Lets play ■

Round and round the garden, like a Teddy Bear...
(childhood rhyme source unknown)

This familiar rhyme, probably played with babies all over the UK, is the kind of rhyme we might use when beginning to handle babies during the daily care and play opportunities – changing, moving, feeding, responding to babies' basics needs with opportunities for games. To begin with these interchanges during which there is play are initiated and introduced by the adult. However, this very quickly changes as babies become aware of the action and activity by the adult and those early handling games. They become the instigator of a play episode by offering a foot or a hand, or gazing at a mobile, which previously the adult has used as a prop for a song or a rhyme. Adults just need to be 'in tune' and the play begins.

## Play it again... ■

Some cultures place a high value on body language and non-verbal exchanges, and in the following observation of Rebecca (10 months) and her key person it is clear that no spoken language or sounds were needed to prompt a repeat of the game.

---

### Boat play

The key worker sat on the floor, legs apart and Rebecca sitting inside them, facing her. She sang the 'Row the boat' song with her. She sang the song and did the actions twice through, and then stopped. Rebecca touched her on the thigh and the key worker responded, 'Again ... you want to sing again?' The singing and moving were repeated, and Rebecca smiled with pleasure.

---

In this play:

- Rebecca is encouraged to use initiative and not be passive;
- Rebecca is helped to be imaginative;
- Her idea to repeat the song is taken up;
- She is experiencing and learning the basics of drama, music and dance;
- Rebecca has an adult who is both responsive and reflective;
- Rebecca is supported in becoming a skilful communicator.

Rebecca was supported to find the rhythm and pace of the game. Both parties carried on, as it was clear both were enjoying themselves. The practitioner's response to the subtle and minute movement of tiny hand reaching for adult and touching gently, asking for more play, indicating that this time she wanted to be part of the play. Rebecca needed this game to be played several times before she was ready to begin to play. Jackson (2002: 389) suggests that:

> holding, handling, stroking and fondling are all considered essential aspects of communication with infants in many pre-literate and non-industrialised societies. And since all babies are born pre-literate and non-industrialised, they probably appreciate the conversation.

Babies use and develop a range of gestures or signs to communicate as they play. This has been developed by some practitioners and parents into programmes of baby signs. Parents use these with babies from about 6 months of age. A television news programme interviewing British parents using one such system highlighted the parents' ability to diminish possible frustration on the babies' part and a heightened awareness by the parents of their babies' subtle signing ability. Parents also admitted to spending more time with their babies to teach them the signs, instead of simply leaving the babies to 'play by themselves'. Perhaps babies are simply responding to greater opportunity for interplay and interaction with their parents.

Jackson (2002) cites studies of babies using the signing system developed by Joseph Garcia which show that seven years on, children who were first taught to sign have a mean IQ of 114 compared with 102 in non-signing babies. Perhaps these babies might have had a higher IQ if their parents had simply spent more time playing with them, playing talking games, tickling toes and bouncing lap games, providing a rich play environment.

## Practice makes...

Everything to do with babies encompasses physical exploration. Play spaces for babies and young children should encourage and promote movement, exploration, reaching for interesting objects, pillows and cushions for playing peep-bo, playing at hiding themselves and toys, clambering over and under. Babies need opportunities to pull themselves up on ballet bars or ladders, interesting items can be hung near or above, not so far that they become a frustration, but situated so that they become part of the play.

With the increasing mobility of society and babies being ferried around from home to early years setting, to supermarket and back to home, babies are spending more and more time immobile. They are strapped into car seats or baby bouncer/rocker-type seats. For some babies these seats are also where they sleep. It also appears that babies are not having frequent opportunities to spend time on their tummies on the floor. All of this constrains play opportunities.

Research into early brain development has confirmed how important crawling is for building strong, dense neural connections. Goddard Blythe (2000) found clear differences in the early development of children who later developed reading, writing and copying difficulties. Many of the children had not crawled, learned to walk later than other children, and were later at learning to talk, ride bikes, catch a ball and carry out fine motor tasks. They had difficulty in sitting still. This indicates that lots of first-hand play experiences are essential for young babies and children. Children who are made to sit still, carry out activities based on worksheets, sit and listen passively, or watch television without an interested adult are unlikely to be creative or imaginative. Nor will they be competent problem-solvers or confident questioners. Babies and young children need lots of opportunity for pretend play and imaginative play.

We know that babies spend less time on the floor than in previous generations, so the essential activity that helps to develop and strengthen head control and cross-crawl movement patterns needed for crawling is being missed. It is through these normal gross motor and fine motor actions during play that the baby's body map is being laid and their spatial awareness is developed.

Practitioners working with very young babies (6–8 weeks of age) can play with the baby whilst developing head control.

- Pop the baby on their tummy and then, doing the same, the practitioner needs to lie on the floor, facing baby.
- Talk or sing to the baby.
- This will help to develop the baby's visual field (eyesight) and neck

muscles, ready for lifting and holding the head up; it is also good for their hearing.
• You can change your position and change the play!


## Choosing resources carefully for movement play ▪

There are many ordinary activities and action games that many parents and practitioners do instinctively with young babies, which we now know can promote brain growth. Parents and practitioners have for centuries rocked babies and children as part of play or to comfort. We now know that regular gentle rocking can help to promote brain growth. Rocking stimulates the vestibular system in the inner ear. The reticular formation is located at the top of the brainstem and its job is to deal with incoming sensory information. The connections from the reticular formation to all the sensory systems mean that it plays a very important part in processing and integrating sensory motor activities. Carter (1999: 23) tells us that the reticular formation matures fully at or after puberty. This area of the brain plays a major role in maintaining attention, it is linked to the vestibular system, which is responsible for coordination and balance, and is very important for maintaining a calm but alert state.

Mogar, Nakahanta and Santos Rico (1999) describe how an underactive vestibular system can lead to hyperactivity and lack of attention. The vestibular system helps to keep the nervous system balanced. Their work in American early years settings challenges conventional approaches to working with children who have difficult behaviour and focuses on experiences that support sensory motor needs and a strong sense of self. They suggest the use of hammocks so that children can swing or spin safely sitting or lying with up to 12 inches floor clearance. The calming effects of being in a (gently) rocking chair – so often used for nursing young babies – or in a hammock induce slow vestibular action. The opposite, the arousing effects of fast vestibular stimulation, are experienced on a rollercoaster ride, or when you swing fast, spinning round and round.

One nursery setting I visited had installed hammocks for the mobile babies and toddlers to crawl into and sleep whenever they wanted to. The hammocks were very low off the ground, but enabled the babies to rock themselves and feel the calming effects of vestibular action. This also encouraged a sense of independence and choice very early on, encouraging mobile babies and young children to make decisions about where they wanted to be, when to play and when to sleep. Some of the nurseries in Reggio Emilia, Italy, visited by a colleague, offer the youngest, only just mobile children opportunities to rest and sleep by providing low-level sleep areas in cubby holes, which the children can access at any time. This shows respect for very young children's rights to be where they want to be, in a 'can get to' environment, encouraging movement through thoughtfully and safely set out play spaces and resources.

Sometimes play needs to be of a relaxing, calming nature. Low hammocks installed in nursery gardens encourage babies and children to harness this naturally soothing and calming activity. They are good for practitioners too. Rocking in a hammock stimulates the vestibular system which controls coordination and balance, which are essential for the development of walking, running, pedalling, being able to run and stop. Play experiences which involve swinging or going on a roundabout can support and enhance sensory motor development.

## Up and away

Once children begin to pull themselves up or cruise round the furniture, many parents choose to use a baby walker. There has been recent research that proves conclusively that these are not helpful to a young child's motor development and can contribute to delay. Atkinson (2003: 7) states that 'baby walkers are dangerous'. She advises that there were 5000 reported accidents involving baby walkers in 1997; babies in the walkers are too young to understand and move away from danger. Accidents have included falling down the stairs or into water and burns and scalds. Young babies, with their relatively large heads, can easily over-balance the baby walker.

Atkinson, a physiotherapist, offers suggestions for better use of time – that babies should be:

- Rolling
- Sitting
- Crawling
- Learning to balance
- Learning to stand

There are many ways of supporting young children to play safely as they begin to become upwardly mobile. It is important to remember that they will want to pull themselves up and cruise round anything that they can reach. Atkinson reminds us that in a baby walker 'children neither sit nor stand and don't use their hands much'. Practitioners need to be inventive and imaginative to support a different type of play now the baby has become mobile. Play that involves different areas of the environment, previously unreachable unless a helpful adult had happened to put you there!

## New places where I want to begin to play

In the photograph we see that Harry has now become a 'cruiser'. He is beginning to pull himself up (and over) and along whatever is to hand. Here he has pulled himself onto the wooden bench; we noticed Harry spending a lot of time on this. He was not playing with any of the resources on the shelf, or in the baskets in the cubby holes. He just seemed to be leaning over, looking at the back of the bench and the floor, until we really looked. The back of the bench is made from heavy-duty card with holes punched in it. Harry was tracing his fingers round and round the holes, pushing his fingers over the holes, really feeling the patterns and textures. He was also running his hand down the back of the bench until he reached the carpet, then tracing his fingers back up again. The practitioners ensured that the bench was available for Harry whilst he continued this aspect of his play.

Harry was in control of his play, choosing and using his own resources. The practitioners extended Harry's play by finding other similar-textured items for him to explore and play with. Several times Harry stretched right over to touch the carpet or toys on the other side, sometimes resulting in a surprisingly slow-motion nose dive. He repeated this, testing out how slowly or quickly he could clear the smooth top of the locker with his tummy!

Even very young children can be supported in their decision-making. Consider this observation:

---

### Puppet play

A group of six toddlers (all between 15 and 18 months) were enjoying puppet and song play with an adult. Not all of the toddlers wanted to be there. A 'subgroup' of three were in the home corner, near to the puppet activity. Later on the subgroup were observed echoing the songs, word for word, and representing the puppet through their own hand movements.

---

The adult was a respectful practitioner, recognizing that the subgroup did not want to be part of the play – they had been invited to join – he had carried on with those who did want the song and

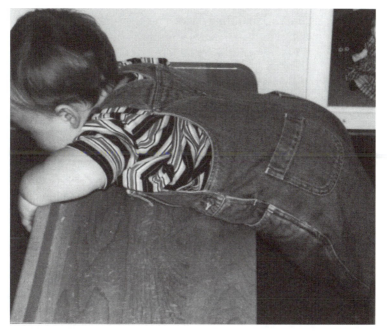

*Harry chooses a place to play.*

puppet play. By being allowed to remain on the edge of the group, still involved with their own play, but listening and watching what was going on with the other children – not wanting to really miss anything – had enhanced these young children's play experience.

As movement develops so too does the opportunity for creative development and pretend play. From making swirling marks in the food on the highchair tray or table, babies and young children move on to playing with sand, cornflour (gloop) and paint, either on the floor or in individual trays. Play with creative materials such as these is just about the sensuousness of the substance as it is squashed in the baby's fist and then smeared or spread across the table or another surface (Matthews 1994).

Practitioners need to be bold enough to offer babies these play opportunities; clearing up is all part of the fun, either in the paddling pool or bath. These experiences can be offered in individual trays on the floor or in a large 'turtle'-type tray for a small group of babies. As the older babies' fine manipulative skills develop through this sort of play, chubby, chunky paintbrushes and objects to make marks with can be offered for easel painting or floor painting – fingers, hands, cotton reels and small knitting cones offer open-ended opportunities for mark-making.

## Tray, table or bath play ▮

The following materials are good:

- jelly
- shaving foam or gel – use the unscented varieties
- bubbles
- finger paint made with starch and gentle soap flakes (the sort used for washing silks and wool, not biological or non-biological machine powders); this forms a substance which feels very similar to gloop – add some food colouring
- dry sand mixed with washing-up liquid and water – becomes lovely and smooth; use with bare hands and feet and treat this as disposable, it does not keep.

Sometimes these experiences are labelled as 'messy play', but to me this term is demeaning to the babies' play experience, and indeed could be why some practitioners and parents view this play as having little value. The tactile pleasure and sensuousness of these materials for babies offer them opportunities to become completely involved and absorbed, using their own movement, their feet and fingers, to feel these materials on bare skin, experience the temperature, cool or warm, the form, liquid or solid, and the texture, slimy or smooth.

## Art, movement and play ▮

Movement and art can become intertwined; very young babies can and need to play with combinations such as gloop, in which solid and fluid become one. Following a visit to nurseries in Reggio Emilia, Italy, where practitioners and professional artists work together with young children, Selleck (1997: 18) cautions readers about 'art activities' for babies and young children. She describes the Italian toddlers playing in the garden after a rain shower. Playing at trail-making in the puddles with long lengths of packaging ribbon, the toddlers strutted, cooed and hooted with excitement as they wore the ribbons tucked into their clothes and watched the intriguing wet/dry patterns created on the paving.

Comparing the Italian toddlers' opportunities for play with 'art activities' she has observed in nurseries in the UK, Selleck tells us: 'I have cringed in observer discomfort as sensual, creative babies, who crave the taste of the porridge glue pots and reach to mouth magazine pictures and paper plates, cope bewilderingly with the nonsense of fixing one to the other' (Selleck 1997: 18). Selleck urges practitioners to consider 'baby art' as being created from the environments of the setting, such as mulchy leaf play, playing in puddles and sunshine, pavement art. She sees baby art as the lines and patterns, arcs and circles in highchair trays of gravy and yoghurt; of the baby's real environment of their experiences, 'gloopy, powdery, watery, pungent sensations of twirls of poo in the potty, sprinkling of talcum for fresh nappies and rain drops tracing down mother's cheeks'. It might be more challenging for practitioners looking after other people's children to consider some of these elements. But mulchy leaf trailing, creating and being patterns in the wet paving, squashing wet, slimy mud through fingers, poking and prodding to create swirls and shapes, seeing the imprint of fingers, hands and feet are all possibilities. Experiences such as Selleck describes cannot fail to inspire practitioners to consider and try some of the elements of true 'baby art'. So 'messy' play should become, and perhaps be called, inspirational play.

## Making connections

Planning for babies' and young children's play means thinking about combinations and connections in babies' and young children's play. In the *English Birth to Three Matters Framework* (2002) the aspect of the child as a Competent Learner, 'Making Connections', promotes and focuses on movement, the environment and using all the senses.

Covering everything up, with paint or gloop, constitutes much of the play at this time. The baby in the *English Birth to Three Matters Framework* (2002) video is enjoying the covering over of the clear perspex as he sits and smears paint across it, first able to see himself and others through the perspex and then in control of the paint and what he sees. There is no need for practitioners to think about an end product. If a parent wants to know what has been happening during the day, and what learning and play has been going on, then a photograph can be taken of the action and an explanation of the play experience can be shared at the end of the day with the parent, explaining the importance of the process and the opportunity for young babies to be in charge of their own play.

*What is this and what can I do with it?*

*What can I do with it?*

## What can I do with this?

Practitioners are very inventive when it comes to offering babies and young children play opportunities. In this series of photographs we see Beth playing with a tin. The practitioners had used the lower part of a notice board to display objects. Beth had reached for the tin at the lowest point of the board, where it was held on with Velcro™. After some initial play – mouthing it, putting her hand inside it, banging and rubbing it – she then put it on the floor and gracefully made the tin roll by using the flat of her palm. I was in the baby room to observe other babies that day and fortunately had my camera to hand.

'Babies and young children learn by doing rather than being told' is one of the principles underpinning the *English Birth to Three Matters Framework (2002)*. Here is Beth beginning to make choices, trying things out and beginning to play.

## Key points from this chapter

- Very young babies and children play, explore and express themselves through movement, some of which is so minute that parents and practitioners caring for other people's children have to be good observers and interpreters;
- The sense of movement of our body is fundamental in the development of self;
- Babies cannot begin to play when they are unsure of the people around them, even though the environment, the routine and equipment are familiar;
- Research has confirmed how important crawling is for building strong, dense neural connections; clear differences in the early physical development and movement of children who later developed literacy difficulties have been identified;
- Rocking in a hammock is helpful for developing strong neurological systems which control coordination and balance, and which are essential for the development of walking, running, pedalling, being able to run and stop;
- Baby walkers are dangerous;
- Babies and young children need movement play opportunities that inspire and create a sense of awe and wonder, using the natural environment;
- Activities that have an end product and are adult-led have no place in the play of babies and very young children;

- Photographs can be taken and an explanation of the play experience can be shared with parents, explaining the importance of the process and the opportunity for young babies to be in charge of their own play.

# 5

# SENSORY PLAY

> Seeing stars it dreams of eternity. Hearing birds it makes music.
> Smelling flowers it is enraptured. Touching tools it transforms
> the earth. But deprived of these sensory experiences, the
> human brain withers and dies.
>
> (Kotulak 1997: 3)

Babies and young children are very sensual beings, touching, tasting,
smelling, hearing, exploring the environment and objects visually,
using sounds to communicate needs, feelings and ideas long before
they have the spoken language of their culture. Babies rely totally on
their senses to begin to tell them about the world around them. It is
through their senses that babies move towards understanding about
the world and begin to construct information and ideas from those
sensory play experiences.

Piaget (1962) called this period the sensorimotor stage, the period
of infancy between birth and 18 months or 2 years, when babies
explore and recognize people and objects, using a combination of
movement and senses; for babies, seeing and feeling the beginnings
of their own movements and actions on objects and people are
fundamental. Very young babies construct schemas (play patterns) of
cause and effect, objects, space and time. Schemas appear as actions,
which become increasingly coordinated and form observable patterns in the children's play (Athey 1990). Babies have tracking,
reaching, grasping and sucking schemas, all related to the way in
which they find out about the world around them.

Think about gentle stroking of bare flesh, recognizing the special
scent of your baby, tickling games, raspberry blowing and other play
exchanges that are sometimes initially greeted with apprehension,
then delight and enjoyment by both giver and receiver. Babies and

young children quickly learn the minutiae of unspoken pauses and gentle pounces, beginning to make sense of complex body language signs through the inter-play and exchanges. Anticipating both the pauses and the pounces, babies and young children giggle or hold their breath in readiness.

The pleasure for a baby in playing naked on the floor, able to play with their toes and experience the different textures of flooring, introduces new play experiences of touch, movement and temperature. Practitioners will need to consider how they offer babies and young children these play experiences in an out-of-home setting, ensuring a respectful, caring play experience. Babies and young children need to have opportunities to play without the constraints of a nappy or clothes. Benjamin, aged 2 years 10 months, newly potty trained and very proud of his 'big boy pants', still loved walking around his and Grandma's house (and garden) without his clothes on whenever possible.

It would appear that rich play experiences such as these are the key to building up memory in very young babies and children, experiences that use a combination of the senses and also need to be repeated over a period of time and involve our emotions.

Torsten Wiesel and David Hubel (in Kotulak 1997: 18), researchers at Harvard Medical School, showed 'that sensory experience is essential for teaching brain cells their jobs'. Their experiments on sewing shut one of a newborn kitten's eyes to test the effect of sensory deprivation led to the discovery that after a few weeks, when the eye was re-opened, the eye could not see. The brain cells normally responsible for processing visual stimulation could not transmit or make the connections necessary to be able to see. However, the other eye, which had not been sewn up, had better vision than normal eyes. The research also led to the discovery that after a 'certain critical period' the brain cells responsible for vision lost the ability to function. This work by Wiesel and Hubel led to debates on brain cells in kittens, other laboratory animals and human beings, and whether there was any connection between young children's brain development and that of animals. A conference in the United States between neuroscientists, educational scientists and psychologists linked up the critical periods in the kittens' brain cell development to that of babies and young children. A debate began on the education and stimulation needed to ensure babies' brain development was not lost to critical periods. This led to a raft of research papers and materials, which in turn fed the hot-housing movement in the United States.

## Critical periods and play

There are, as I discovered when researching play resources for young children under 3, a range of websites, toys, books and materials on the market extolling these 'critical periods' of early brain development, and selling the wonders of educational materials from flash cards to videos for babies less than a year old to watch and learn from. This has not contributed to education and learning by promoting the need to immerse very young babies and children in particular activities or risk failing their intellectual development, rather than supporting play.

Meltzoff (in Gopnik, Meltzoff and Kuhl 1999) spoke about how some people in the toy and educational market were using the neuroscientists' work to endorse products and inform parents about boosting their baby's brains through music, flash cards and toys. He reminded us that babies need us to do normal things with them – talk, play, 'mess about', and most of all spend time with them. It is important that practitioners are able to discuss and debate with parents the importance of reflecting on what babies need.

Blakemore (1998, 2000) argues that the brain passes through 'sensitive periods', and that these are flexible, that there probably are periods when there is sensitivity to a particular kind of learning, such as learning to talk, to read or to be sociable. Wiesel concluded that very young children should be living in an enriched sensory environment. Music to early practitioners ears.

Wiesel and Hubel discovered that the brain is able to reduce experiences from the world into bite-sized chunks relating to all of our sensory experiences, which are in turn sent as electrochemical signals to be stored in particular parts of the brain as information about sensory input – colour, smell, movement, sound, light and touch. Our brain then breaks up and stores images in specialized areas, and the connections between groups of cells are used to capture and store all the elements of an experience – the smell or the touch of a material.

The young brain needs these rich sensory play experiences to build up the neural connections and begin the hard-wiring of the brain; of that there appears to be agreement among the neuroscientists, the child's environment plays a big part in shaping and producing physical changes in the developing brain. It is how we as educationalists and practitioners interpret and use this knowledge to ensure that young children have access to a play-led, multisensory learning environment that is the key focus now.

## Playing and bathing in good experiences

Let's consider why memories are important, and especially what sort of experiences we should be ensuring our very young children have through their play.

As adults we can't remember things that happened to us before the age of 3; this is because the hippocampus in the brain, where memories begin, is not fully developed. However, certain emotional memories may be stored in the amygdala, a part of the limbic system, which controls emotions and drives. The amygdala tells us what we should avoid and reminds us of things that are frightening or unpleasant, like phobias and flashbacks. It picks up and responds to expressions of fear, facial expressions and tone of voice. Babies respond to facial expressions from birth, responding appropriately, although this improves as the frontal lobes of the cortex, the emotional area of the brain, mature. There appears to be a link between an abnormal amygdala and the inability to sense emotion in other people, behaviour displayed, for example, by psychopaths. Some scientists link this to brain damage, but others think that it may be due to lack of bonding between mothers and babies. Classic signs such as emotional coldness, bullying, deceit and lack of remorse are all attributed to amygdala malfunction (Carter 1999: 93).

Babies need and respond well to being closely bonded with, by being touched and talked to. All play experiences give reassurance and confidence, decreasing the amount of stress and the stress hormone, cortisol, being made and released into the brain. Early exposure to stress and violence, whether received or observed, appears to have a negative effect on very young children's brain development. Attachment relationships that do not work out can then affect brain development. Positive attachment relationships, building on close communication through touch and sharing play experiences, are essential for young babies and children.

Steele (2001) reminded practitioners that every aspect of a baby's brain development can be thrown off if one of their base attachment relationships goes very wrong. Violence or emotional neglect in the first three years can distort or change the neural pathways. Instead of being alert for learning, babies who have experienced serious detachments have a predisposition to fight or flight, the adrenalin response, which should only occur when real danger is apparent. The growth and development of the brains of babies and young children who have had violent experiences, such as domestic violence or being smacked, may be affected by those experiences, constraining the possibility for play. The neural pathways are deepened by the experiences and babies appear to be always on the look-out for the next frightening experience; unlike the rest of us whose emergency response signals respond when needed, these babies and young children always appear to be 'on the edge', waiting for something to happen. Play is not possible under these conditions. Steele (2001) also reported that children who were insecure or disoriented in a 'strange situation' still had raised cortisol levels up to half an hour after reunion with the parent.

## Looking at the senses: smell, touch, vision, taste, hearing

### *Smell*

The reason why the sense of smell is so powerfully linked to memory is that our olfactory system is associated with the limbic system of the brain, the area that deals with emotions and memory.

Smell can trigger memories of particular personal experiences; cut grass reminds some of us of those summery childhood days, but what about smell which reminds us of people or events long since forgotten – my husband tells me of a scent, the name of which he can't recall, but whenever he smells it, he is reminded of a workplace experience when as a young catering student he and several others had to cook and serve silver service style in the home of a middle-aged couple. The perfume was worn by the lady of the house, and the scent of this particular perfume reminds him of this day; even though the actual event was long forgotten, the perfume helped him piece it together again, and he could even begin to remember the other students with him that day.

We know that babies recognize and discriminate smells at only a few hours old. I was a very young nursery nurse working in the baby unit when MacFarlane's (1975) research was carried out into baby's olfactory systems at the John Radcliffe Maternity Unit. The mothers' breast milk was soaked onto a pad, and the babies responded only to the scent of their own mother's milk, by turning towards the familiar smell.

So we know that newborns already have a well-developed sense of smell. Our sense of smell may not be used as much as it should, and yet it is so clearly linked to memory, to help us to gain new information, and as we have already noted, to discriminate between people or places. Smell is also very closely linked to taste and the brain uses the two together very often, giving us an improved sensation.

---

### Playing with our noses

In the baby room, bunches of fresh lavender can be hung around the sleeping area; lavender is known for its restful qualities.

For the treasure basket, a fresh fruit such as a lemon, an orange or a lime are all the right sort of size for small hands to explore and encourage babies to use their noses as they play.

- Check them for freshness.
- Avoid ready scented objects for the treasure basket as these may contain oils that should not be ingested – remember everything goes into mouths!

---

For non-mobile babies small cushions with lavender, cinnamon or mint can be added to the cushion corner. Toddlers can be encouraged to smell the cushions and be given the names for the scents. Make scented mobiles to keep the baby rooms free from artificial and harsh scents of disinfectant or air freshener. The home base can become a sniffers' delight, with fresh flowers, or seasonal scented plants such as hyacinth, freesias, pots of scented herbs; little baskets can hold small material bags of lavender, sage, mint, lemon mint; or baskets with a nutmeg, cinnamon sticks, vanilla pods. Avoid aromatherapy oils with babies and toddlers as these can have powerful ill-effects if used without expert knowledge.

These suggestions will require close adult supervision. Make sure you are aware of any allergies or sensitivities. By including families in the setting's play experiences, with an invitation for them to contribute to the wonderful array of scents available, you will improve the experience for the children and include scents that are special to your children and their community.

### *Touch*

Almost everything involving babies and young children involves touch. Babies rely totally on others to move them, bring things to them and do almost everything for them. From birth the newborn is held, checked over by the midwife, perhaps touched by this person, but most importantly will be touched by and be touching his new parents.

Murray and Andrews (2000: 22) show the first few minutes of Ethan's life, how he comforts himself, when not even a minute old, by finding his thumb and putting it in his mouth. He is moved for a check over, and cries as he is briefly left uncovered, having lost his thumb which he had been sucking. He is reunited with his mother, and through careful touching and containing of his thrashing arms he is stroked and calmed by his mother. All this in the first minute of his life; touching then – knowing how to touch, when to touch – is important and something that most adults do instinctively.

We touch our babies to tell them what we are doing or what is about to happen. They are touched as we change, feed and bathe them; we touch them for pleasure, both given and received, stroking the soft newborn flesh of yet another miracle; babies and children touch us to find out who we are, where we begin, what we are made of and how we are part of them; later we touch to heal and reassure, 'kiss it better', soothing the pain of a grazed knee and damaged pride when the child's developing co-ordination and two wheels meet!

---

### Hello play

Benjamin, aged 3 months, was sitting on his mother's knee. Lily, aged 21 months, one of his older sisters, was also cuddled in close by. Benjamin began waving his arm around, prodded and poked Lily in the ear. Michaela gently took Benjamin's hand and making stroking movements on Lily's face, reassured Lily that he didn't know how to hurt people, helped Benjamin to say 'hello' to Lily and let him continue to stroke her face.

---

Touch involves the whole body; babies and young children use their hands, lips, tongue, mouth and feet to touch people and objects to find out about this strange world they have become part of. As they touch they are finding out about their own body, where they begin and end, learning to judge distance as they stretch out to touch another face. Babies' faces, tummies, hands and soles of their feet are very sensitive: I observed babies using the soles of their feet to play with and find out more about objects in the treasure basket.

Babies in group care need to be positioned carefully so that they have enough space for their own body movements as they play, still able to touch each other; however, we need to intercept gently and help them as through playful exploration they inadvertently offer a friendly poke.

Playing with tactile objects, human or otherwise, takes a lot of time and babies and young children need the opportunity to really have visually 'sized up' an object before they begin to touch and play with it. This can sometimes lead to practitioners thinking that certain

**Foot play**

Harry was at the treasure basket, his feet playing with a large, flat shell, beautifully smooth with mother of pearl on the inside and rough, deeply layered on the other. As he played with an upturned pot with his hands, Harry's feet were playing with the shell. One foot fitted inside the smooth area and he drew his foot backwards and forwards around the interior of the shell. He drew his feet together around the shell and then lifted the shell up and down with his feet, bringing it closer to his body. He then began to use his hands to stroke the shell.

Cerys was playing alone at the treasure basket. She finds a wooden foot roller in the basket and drops it in between her legs. After a while she finds the roller again, this time with her feet. She uses the soles of her feet to move the roller up and down rhythmically. Her feet appear to become an extension of herself as she stretches her arms, legs and tummy. She smiles at the near-by adult. She is making sounds, which appear to describe the pleasure of the movement. The roller is moved on the floor using the sole of one foot and in between her two feet; the pleasure seems to be about Cerys' whole body movement, not just the rolling of the roller. She keeps the roller in between her feet, playing with it for more than 10 minutes, she then returns to the basket.

*Learning for practitioners here:* Harry had socks on during these observations; Cerys was bare footed. We made it a rule to ensure that socks were always removed when babies were seated at the treasure basket.

objects are of no interest and being moved away. Careful observations will show whether the child is interested. My observations of the treasure basket showed that Harry, Cerys and Alice all had favourite items, which they returned to every time the basket was offered. Even if they did not explore them for long, the object was kept within touching distance, often wedged near a leg. During the study I did not remove any items from the basket unless they had become unusable; however it is essential to ensure that the treasure basket, like all resources, is carefully replenished when items are no longer safe, or too chewed, or simply not being played with.

Babies and young children need time to do this sizing up, they need time to practise the movements essential for grabbing and grasping objects for further play. This needs to be repeated, so that the baby or young child can build up the knowledge that comes through playing with objects in similar and different ways, a grab with either hand eventually results in the object coming closer.

Play materials such as a treasure basket can offer seated babies opportunities to play with a range of interesting objects, with many materials, textures and shapes. Babies and young children need three-dimensional objects – blocks, jugs, saucepans, boxes and containers of different sizes – things that can contain other objects, objects to be contained.

### Please do touch

For many babies and young children, frequent negatives such as 'don't touch' or 'shall we move this out of your way' can be disheartening. Babies rely totally on us when they are unable to move to make safe selections, and we should offer them all sorts of interesting things that they can touch.

Once a young child is on the move, the world becomes a far more interesting place for exploration. It is up to us to ensure that the environments we create for young mobile children are challenging, interesting and as safe as possible. You only need to accompany a toddler on a walk to see what is so interesting about the world; everything we miss is at the child's level. Cracks in walls or on the pavement could house all manner of things, dead and alive, and little fingers or even a hand can go in to find out exactly what is going on. Practitioners will need to bear in mind that everyday routines of walking or crawling to another area of the setting should involve lengthy explorations and discussions of the route and the people on the way.

### Vision

Murray and Andrews (2000: 88) demonstrate how objects that have strong, clear lines, black and white patterns of stripes, circles or checks, captivate babies. We see Emily, aged 1 week, tracking a black and white lollipop and holding it in her view. She watches for several minutes, stretches an arm towards the lollipop and then clearly signals 'had enough' by turning away. We know that babies prefer visually complex patterns, and that this complexity probably links with their developing acuity. It is a time when we can ensure that we offer babies the sort of play that will support the physical development of perception and visual awareness.

*Photo tins*

In some of the nurseries I worked in we introduced photo tins. Using formula milk tins, cover them with photographs of the child's parents or carers. Laminate the photos or cover the tin with clear Fablon℠. These make personal picture books for the baby and have the added advantage of being mobile, as Beth discovered earlier in the book. Very young babies can enjoy the photo tin, as they lie on their tummies – essential for developing muscles and posture. But watch as they look closely at photographs of people that they know well. You can vary this with other familiar and relevant pictures. Have pictures and photographs of the real people and families (with their permission) from your setting displayed at vision level for all babies and children.

It is useful sometimes to lie on the floor and test out whether pictures, mirrors, and so on are placed appropriately for babies and toddlers to be of any use. There are also ranges of unbreakable, wipeable frames. Real artists' work, modern and contemporary, can also be very appropriate for baby and toddler areas. Find prints that interest the children and frame them, again at baby viewing height – some at 'lying on the floor height', to those at 'just able to pull myself up and have a look at this' height. Imaginative practitioners will ensure that there are simple handles or bars made available for babies and toddlers to pull themselves up with and hold on to.

*Mobiles*

Consider the alternatives to manufactured mobiles. By making your own you can enhance the individual baby's play. If you have hooks in the ceiling or on a rack suspended from the ceiling, you can ring the changes and give the babies something different to look at. Here are some tried and tested ideas:

- budgie or 'cow' bells, Indian bells attached to ribbon and suspended at different lengths;
- CDs threaded to hang vertically or horizontally;
- black, white, red, plain and patterned discs, suspended at an appropriate height.

Do ensure that anything hanging is secured safely and that babies cannot hurt themselves or other babies as they kick or swing the mobiles.

## *Taste*

Babies and young children take everything to their mouths. Watch a new baby as his or her fist finds its way into their mouth, how your shoulder is always sucked when holding a baby, and everything about you is explored by mouth ... we are our babies' first plaything and probably the most interesting! There are four aspects to taste – sweet, sour, bitter and salt. We know that newborn babies can distinguish between sweet and sour, and show pleasure at a sweet smell and disgust at something like rotten eggs, so already they are able to discriminate between two out of the four main taste sensations.

Longhorn (1988), working with children with complex needs, describes how taste and smell are very closely linked; subconsciously we smell everything before we taste it, and the odour (which is information) from the delicious oven-baked bread on our plate is transmitted to the brain. The sense of smell, combined with the taste buds in the mouth, helps us to appreciate flavour and taste to the full. Play experiences encouraging sensory awareness, such as tasting tables, can encourage young children to become multisensory. Offering a combination of fruit or vegetables, such as fresh, ripe peaches or nectarines, are visually appealing, smell heavenly and then taste like – well, fresh nectarines! Longhorn (1988) describes how to offer a 'taste curriculum' to children with special needs. However, as she points out, a sensory curriculum (p.18) is appropriate right across the spectrum, at different times in the lives of adults and children, from babies who are dependent on learning through their senses and including those with sensory deprivation, either permanent or temporary, through illness or injury. A sensory curriculum can be planned to be an integral part of the curriculum for children with special needs, not seen as an added extra, but meeting the needs of the individual child.

We can ensure through everyday good routines that babies and young children enjoy sensory experiences, bringing together aspects of the *English Birth to Three Matters Framework* (2002) in everyday events.

---

### Encouraging healthy choices, being together, growing and developing

At lunchtime a plate of freshly prepared fruit was placed on the table; the babies had watched the staff prepare the fruit and been included in the discussion about what was on the plate. The babies and toddlers were encouraged to select their own piece of fruit from the plate. A tiny portion of fruit was given to each child to try out. Several babies showed they wanted more. The practitioner slowly passed the plate round all the children. The babies and toddlers all helped themselves or helped others to take more fruit, selecting from the variety on the plate.

These babies and toddlers were being encouraged to:

- become decision-makers, demonstrating individual pre-ferences;
- use their developing physical coordination;
- explore different tastes, smells and textures;
- be well nourished;
- be part of a group, sharing and enjoying lunch – not a rushed part of the daily routine to be got over as quickly as possible.

---

Mouthing is very important for young babies. By playing with objects in their mouth, babies begin to put together and store information about the object. Even very young babies do this. Thinking about the following piece of research, what interesting objects can you offer to enable babies to safely mouth and learn about their world?

### What kind of dummy?

Andrew Meltzoff (in Gopnik, Meltzoff and Kuhl 1999) gave babies aged 1 month a dummy to suck. The dummies were either lumpy or smooth and not seen by the baby. The babies were then shown pictures of lumpy or smooth objects, but they were not able to touch them. They looked for longer at the image of the object that was the same shape as the one they had been sucking.

Babies were recognizing and discriminating between objects; they can relate the feel of an object to what it looks like. Babies begin to learn about size, density, texture. They also begin to remember things related to objects and actions.

## Listening and sounds ◾

Sound is considered in detail in Chapter 9.

## Key points from this chapter ◾

- Babies and young children are very sensual beings;
- Through multisensory play experiences, babies move from understanding about the world and begin to construct information;
- Smell and memory are linked because the olfactory system is part of the limbic system of the brain, the area that deals with emotions and memory;
- Practitioners need to make sure that they offer safe smelling experiences for babies and young children in out-of-home settings;
- Babies prefer visually complex patterns. Practitioners will need to ensure that babies are offered play experiences that will support the physical development of perception and visual awareness;
- A multisensory curriculum is appropriate at different times in the lives of adults and children, from babies who are dependent on learning through their senses and those with sensory deprivation, either permanent or temporary, through illness or injury;
- A sensory curriculum can be planned to be an integral, inclusive part of the curriculum for all children, not seen as an added extra, but meeting the needs of the individual child.

# 6

# TREASURE BASKETS

Babies use their five senses along with their co-ordination of
eye and hand in playing with objects, which in their various
ways offer them a rich stimulus.

(Goldschmied 1989: 9)

## What is a treasure basket?

Elinor Goldschmied conceived the idea of the treasure basket, using
her many observations whilst working with babies in full-time care
environments in Italy and the UK. The treasure basket was in
response to observations of babies exploring and playing with objects
from the real world, the things that we all recognize young children
are always interested in – bunches of keys, packaging, baking tins and
wooden spoons.

Goldschmied (1994: 97) recommends that a basket should be not
less than 14 inches in diameter and 4 to 5 inches high, without a
handle and having a flat bottom. She suggests straight sides and that
it is made of a natural material. A circular basket is easier for seating
three babies around, and for a willow-woven basket it is essential that
all the ends are safely woven in. We will play with and explore the
contents of a basket later in the chapter.

Goldschmied's observations were about the rapidly changing and
developing play needs of young babies, as they spend more time
awake and can begin to be propped up to see the world from another
angle. This is the time to think about the baby's developing hand–
eye–object control, and offer a variety and range of objects for them
to play with. Goldschmied observed that babies spent more time

playing with objects not normally considered as playthings. These objects tended to be from the real or natural world, with a range of textures and those that stimulate the senses of smell, hearing and taste.

Goldschmied (1989: 9) observed that a baby's capacity for concentration is the most striking feature of early play, and I agree with her. However, this is usually overlooked, or not even considered as a feature of early play, by many practitioners.

During training sessions when I have shared my videos of babies playing at a treasure basket, the initial surprise of practitioners when we note the time babies have spent at individual objects or at the basket never amazes me. It appears that some practitioners who do not use the basket to its full potential never see the concentration or perseverance of babies as they explore and begin to play. Once practitioners have participated in a training session and been introduced to a well-thought-through basket and contents, their attitude to collecting, organizing and offering the basket in their settings usually changes.

*A basket full of treasure.*

The treasure basket is a basket piled high with objects safely and specifically chosen by an adult. The basket is for babies who are able to sit, either with or without support, from approximately 6 to 9 months of age, when their eye–hand–mouth coordination is at that continually developing stage; sitting at the basket gives opportunities for practising this. The objects encourage maximum use of all the senses and the baby is allowed to choose and explore the objects in their own time and at their own pace. So they are able to rummage, select, try out (by mouthing, smelling, touching and staring intently) and discard objects. At its most complex, the basket allows us to observe babies using cognitive skills such as memory, reasoning and problem-solving. Babies are able to choose whether to play and explore an object or not, how long they stay with it, and how to explore it – with eyes, mouth, hands or toes.

## Meeting Elinor Goldschmied

Elinor Goldschmied is one of Europe's most respected and acknowledged experts on day care. Her work with very young children based on practice and observations has led to the development of training material for nursery practitioners. The focus of her work has been on the treasure basket and heuristic play, and the 'key person approach'.

When I first met Elinor Goldschmied, she told me that she 'Wanted to weep or have a temper tantrum at some of the "treasure baskets" that she had been asked to look at when visiting nurseries.' Some were too small, others were too big, so that babies would not be able to lean in safely and reach or play with the objects. Some baskets held only a few items. I showed her my own treasure basket with some trepidation. Her reaction, to my relief, was sheer delight and she was just like an inquisitive child as she delved into the basket – 'What have you got? Let me see, let me touch, let me play!'

We exchanged an item from each other's baskets; I gave her a small wooden rattle in the shape of a dovecote containing two beads in the cote part. It is a very sensuous piece of wood, smooth, beautifully shaped and the wooden beads make a satisfying yet gentle sound. The rattles are also available with bells in the cote, altering the sound. Offering babies objects that appear to be the same but are different helps them to become selective. Goldschmied gave me a green glass miniature brandy bottle from the old GWR trains' buffet car. I had a clear glass miniature jam pot in my basket. We had discussed and debated the pros and cons relating to health and safety with glass.

Those working with other people's children need to exercise caution in this. Any glass object put in a treasure basket needs to be examined extremely carefully to test that it cannot be chewed and broken with a determined baby's jaw and gums. Many items of modern glass are too fragile for a treasure basket and will not stand up to the rigours of being pushed around the basket and banged against other solid heavy objects in the basket. Health and safety must always come first when selecting objects for the basket, and this is discussed at length later on.

## Respecting babies through choosing objects for their play

One of Goldschmied's guiding principles is that the contents of the treasure basket should be 'beautiful'; she told me:

> … if you put a common object in the treasure basket it has to be a very good one, not inferior, otherwise the treasure basket becomes the rubbish basket, and that is why a badly collected treasure basket is the worst possible advertisement because it denigrates something which could be, should be appreciated – therefore it's got to be safe, it's got to be beautiful.

I had had a willow basket hand made, following the guidance in Goldschmied's book. Her surprise and delight was because I was the first person she had met to have a 'proper' basket made. The size and shape of the basket are vital. After many observations, Goldschmied has worked out the size to ensure eye–hand–object coordination is enabled. The basket is deep enough for babies to reach over and into, but will not tip as it has a flat bottom. On several occasions during our conversations, Goldschmied returned to the importance of ergonomically correct equipment, for both babies (and children) and the adults who work with them. She was especially concerned with changing tables and caring for practitioners' backs. She is interested in the Alexander Technique and has worked with physiotherapists and occupational therapists on equipment that is fit for purpose.

I had wanted to have a 'proper' basket made as many of the baskets I had seen being used in early years settings were inappropriate for babies. They were either too deep, like laundry baskets or too shallow, poor-quality weave and with pieces of willow or cane dangling or sharp to babies' hands. I also have very strong principles in that I think we should look very carefully as to the makers and sources of equipment. Cheap imported baskets are available, but there are ethical considerations in this. I met Roy Youdale, a Master Craftsman, at a craft fair and saw some of his hand-woven willow baskets. We met again and I described to him the sort of thing I wanted, and gave him the measurements from Goldschmied's book. I tested out

*Basket and rattles made of willow.*

several prototypes, Roy used various weaving techniques for the base of the basket to ensure that the willow did not come undone, and a final design was made. We added a rim to the final design as my observations showed that the babies using the 'rimmed prototype' used the rim quite adeptly to balance objects on and as a resting point before lifting the object to their chest or face. A treasure basket design was made. Roy has also made willow rattles, which have been enjoyed by babies and adults alike.

The basket Roy created at my request has the following specifications:

• Circumference: 14 inches

- Depth: 4 inches
- Made from different natural-coloured willows – green, black, red, ochre
- Has a lip

I wanted to know what had influenced Goldschmied and how the treasure basket had come to fruition. Goldschmied spent her early childhood growing up in Gloucestershire. It sounded an idyllic time, being left to play alone and with her older brothers. They played in mud-banks by the river, making mud-pies, tree-houses and dens. Using all the natural things around them, they played, making boats from walnut shells and pine cones to float down the stream. One of her earliest memories was that of a rag doll called Tom. They had no real toys, and although the adults knew where the children were, they spent summers and winters outdoors. She remembers an environment of 'calm' within which 'time seemed really limitless'. This was where her earliest memories of making her own 'collections' began. It seemed to me that her childhood was about free flow play (Bruce 1991).

Goldschmied's working background is in education and psychiatric social work (as it was known at the time). The treasure basket was developed whilst she was working in Italy in the early 1950s with a group of teenage mothers and their babies. These girls were not in an institution in the medical sense of the word, but in 'villaggio della madre e fanciullo', or community for mother and child, where Goldschmied worked for 10 years. This was followed by the development of a nursery in Milan. The mothers in the 'villaggio' remained with their children, which was a pioneering approach at the time, in total contrast to the then usual process of removing babies and ostracizing mothers.

Goldschmied ran the nursery to support the mothers who were living with their babies, some of whom were completing their education, or returning to education. To rebuild their own lives, which had been devastated by the blame and despair socially at that time, was a struggle. The focus for Goldschmied was always, how can the relationship of mother and baby be fostered, maintained and encouraged? The mothers needed to understand a baby's developing needs and Goldschmied worked as part of a team to identify and provide the support they needed.

The treasure basket was something Goldschmied had always wanted to do; she had had the idea for some time, wanting to look to and use the environment as a natural resource, where objects from the real world were of more value to a baby's play. This period in Italy gave her the opportune moment to try it out. The treasure basket evolved as a collection of items for the babies to explore, as there were no 'toys' and the young mothers were encouraged to bring things to the nursery for Goldschmied's basket. It was an emerging culture, grounded in poverty. However, the best for the baby was not generally considered something they could pick up from the path or woods. Relatives, aunts and mothers were shocked by the idea; they would much prefer, as Goldschmied describes it, to give the baby 'something brightly coloured and useless'. The nursery was using a valueless basket, considered insulting by a society at that time coming out of the poverty of war. The symbolism of achievement involved giving colourful gifts. An understanding of the cultural contexts in which this was offered was essential. Goldschmied and her team worked gradually, developing trust and dialogue with the mothers, and sharing the understanding of babies' needs. Everything in the basket, no matter how ordinary, had to be clean, beautiful and safe.

Goldschmied's observations in the Italian nurseries, where, as in other countries during this period, babies were reared without individualized care, were of infants who were very anxious, withdrawn and unable to make contact with new or strange objects. They did not even try to touch attractive toys. The babies would 'timidly put out a hand and withdraw'. Goldschmied's subsequent work to change the relationships of adults working with babies, developing closer contact with them, was influenced by the research of John Bowlby (1907–1990). His work showed that babies need the close emotional contact of an adult in order to explore objects. This led to the development of the 'key person approach'. Goldschmied also designed and made play equipment for the nurseries, some of which is still in place today.

## Basket play

As they begin to play with a treasure basket, the babies are able to test out the objects. Will it move? Is it noisy, hard, soft, cold, warm or hot? Are any of these constant? Once babies are able to sit unsupported, they get a new sense of autonomy, to see things around them from a different perspective, and to be able to have a degree of control over objects and events. However, sitting also brings frustrations. Interesting things seem to be out of reach or prohibited from further exploration by adults saying 'no' or 'don't touch'. The 'objects' in the treasure basket are not toys in the conventional sense but playthings that babies might have access to once they are more mobile and able to satisfy their own curiosity. In face, they are probably the sort of objects that would be greeted with 'no' or 'don't touch' from most adults, practitioners and parents.

Many parents looking at a treasure basket for the first time observe with horror that most of the contents are not those that they would initially choose to give their baby to explore – no toys, no recognizable 'baby things'. However, as we will discover shortly when we look at a parents' evening and the comments made, with some positive, first-hand experience and opportunities to play initial prejudices can be challenged and changed.

Babies and toddlers find it almost impossible not to touch and handle everything they come across, despite anxious adults telling them not to 'fiddle'. Some adults use the word 'play' in a derogatory sense – 'stop playing about with that' when something is being touched, explored. Some adults still need to touch objects to find out about or confirm their thinking on the size, shape and textures. We all have different learning styles; some of us are auditory learners, some visual or kinaesthetic. Research on learning styles (Rodd 1998) appears to show that very young children do display preferred learning styles and that the youngest children favour kinaesthetic approaches to learning, followed by visual and auditory styles.

## Family connections, personal learning

I realized that I had made a 'treasure basket' of sorts for my son, long before I first read Goldschmied's chapter 'Play and learning in the first year of life' (1989). We had a 'bit box' in which I kept items (now in my treasure basket) which Alistair enjoyed exploring and which certainly kept him busy for long enough periods, enabling me to finish and enjoy a cup of tea. At the time, this seemed a good enough reason to search out those things he was interested in. These included a glass paperweight, always cool, heavy, and curious because it held a beautiful flower, which was unreachable, no matter which way the glass was turned and mouthed. The weight was no deterrent to his play, grasping it securely with both hands, using his hands and his chest to support the paperweight as he rolled it up to his mouth for further playing with his tongue and gums. Pine cones, collected on pram-pushing expeditions or baby carrier walks, were always of interest (washed under the hot tap first), and pebbles, keys, and some beautifully turned pieces of wood all added to his first play experiences.

Without the benefit of Goldschmied's observations, I also ensured I stayed close to Alistair as he played with the bit box, mindful that none of these playthings were meant for the purposeful exploration his inquisitive 7-month-old brain was giving them, but somehow knowing that my son was engaged in a complex activity. He was not a 'grizzly' baby, perhaps due to my 'tuned-in-ness' of ensuring he had lots of conversations, being part of what was going on around him and not simply an onlooker, and, naturally, having many interesting objects from the real world to play with. All of which led to many hours of concentrated play, with no need for 'entertainment' from me. I was able to enjoy his play and delight at the new objects offered for his bit box. Today, at the age of 20, he approaches new tools and objects with ease and explores them skilfully, assessing their useful-ness with dexterity and confidence.

My daughter Laura inherited the bit box, which had grown con-siderably, and she also enjoyed rummaging through baskets or con-tainers of objects, taking pleasure in the tactile experience and the scent, particularly of natural objects and those of a more unusual nature from the real world. She still searches out and saves things that might be nice for our young nephew and nieces (aged 3, 5, and 7) to play with or useful for my training sessions!

## Plastic toys versus real

> A short meditation on plastic, often pondered as I play with a plethora of ... Doesn't it come in neutral colours?
>
> (Candappa 2001: 40)

Playing with objects is not simply for 'amusement' or to be seen as an 'activity'; the treasure basket can be a powerful medium through which babies can safely play with the sorts of objects they would probably choose for themselves if they were mobile enough or had the dexterity to reach them. Think about the baby persistently trying to grab the car keys or interested in whatever is making a noise in a handbag, or the chain around your neck.

Goldschmied (1986: 9) advocates a treasure basket in which none of the objects are 'toys', or made of plastic. She considers plastic to have very little value in the world of babies exploring.

It is possible to argue here that plastic objects can provide some degree of interest. I have a collection of textured balls that I have used with babies as they do offer tactile experiences – some of them are spiky, some have ridges and some are raised. Ranges of scented balls also offer new experiences for babies. The use of plastics based on PVC has caused concern, a report in 1999 indicating that philates, a component part of plastic, may be carcinogenic led to some con-cern amongst users and manufacturers of children's toys. Many manufacturers have removed or reduced the philates content. A baby born and brought up in the Western world today will probably have had many experiences of plastic, from feeding time to travel, to baby gyms and rattles, by the time they reach 6 months old. We need to begin to look for alternatives to plastic and reduce the exposure to plastic such young children have.

## Treasured objects

Goldschmied (1989) identifies a list of objects for a treasure basket, which was revised in 1994 and 2000. Using Goldschmied's headings for guidance, the objects I have collected for my basket are listed in Table 6.1. This is by no means an exhaustive list, nor should practitioners simply use it as a tick list for selecting their own objects. Once you start collecting, objects can be found in all kinds of places, and other people will begin to collect and save objects for your basket – I have just returned from a holiday where I found the perfect tea infuser for my basket! Many colleagues have also added to my basket over the years; now it holds personal memories of practitioners and settings in addition to those memories of my children's treasures.

## A healthy child and the treasure basket

When selecting items for the treasure basket, it is important to avoid painted objects, especially when you are unsure of the origin of the object. Many imported goods are not subject to the same legislation as in the UK on the lead content of paint, so objects from exotic holiday locations or any you are unable to verify the paint content of are best not included in the treasure basket. Any object with sharp edges and lose parts should be avoided. Objects need to be regularly checked and replaced – shells become cracked or chipped and can cut delicate skin. Objects that have had artificial scents added, such as scented shaped turned items of wood, lemons, apples, and so on, also need to be avoided because all of these items will be sucked and mouthed by the babies. Far better to have various naturally scented pieces of turned wood and real fruit (replaced regularly) such as a lemon, lime, and orange.

The whisk in my basket is an extremely solid piece of metal and has no moving parts, unlike some of the cheap whisks available for whisking milky drinks. Mine was quite expensive – but my husband was a chef and hasn't missed this lovely little whisk from his collection! There are similar whisks where the balloon is made of

**Table 6.1** *Personal treasures*

| Objects made of natural materials: | Natural objects: | Wooden objects: |
|---|---|---|
| Small shoe brush | Fir cones – different sizes | Small boxes, lined |
| House paint brush | Corks, large size | Curtain rings – different sizes |
| Shaving brush | Cork block | Clothes pegs, dolly peg type |
| Woollen ball | Dried gourd | Egg cup |
| Willow rattles | Sea grass pear | Small turned bowl |
| Napkin ring made from horn | Piece of loofah | Cylinders, cotton reels |
| Nest of baskets and lids – five sizes | Shells – various sizes | Turned wooden eggs |
| Small raffia container | | Foot massager |
| | | Nut cracker |
| **Objects in other materials:** | | Bobbin |
| Leather purse with popper – old Brownie purse! | | Honey dipper |
| Purse with clip fastener | **Metal objects:** | Two wooden rattles – with beads/bells |
| Coloured marble egg | Set of measuring spoons | Toadstool darner |
| High bouncer ball | Brass curtain rings on a ring | Lemon squeezer |
| Stress ball | Metal egg cup | Wooden ball |
| Length of rubber tubing | Small balloon whisk | Pastry brush |
| Rubber coasters | Small tins | Small turned bowl |
| Leather spectacle case | Round reflective lids | |
| Small knitted teddy | Bunch of keys | **Paper, cardboard:** |
| Bath plug with chain | Flat hexagonal tin | Greaseproof paper, scrunched up |
| Small cloth bags with thyme, rosemary, cloves | Individual moulds | Small cardboard boxes |
| Bean bag | Oval tea-leaf strainer | Soft corrugated paper |
| Ceramic lid | | Small paper gift-type bags with cord handles |
| Perfume top | | |
| Acrylic wine stopper | | |
| Satin-lined velvet ring box | | |
| Organza bag | | |
| Velvet bow tie | | |
| Small pieces of various fabrics | | |
| Paperweight – acrylic, flat | | |
| Florist's cube | | |

separate wires held together. These are not safe for babies or toddlers to mouth as they come apart easily. Check for safety – the only sort to include in the basket are those with a completely moulded handle and whisk, no moving parts or parts able to be separated. If in doubt – leave it out!

As Goldschmied and Jackson advise (1994: 95), there are many items that are suitable for a treasure basket, so if you have any doubts about the suitability of an item or its safety, 'throw it out'. Goldschmied lists 93 items, not all of which I would personally put in a treasure basket. I suggest caution with the suggestion of lengths of chain – I attached mine securely to a bath plug and the babies' pleasure in playing with this was very evident. Chain comes in different link sizes and weights, so caution and common sense must prevail as babies and toddlers will also put these into the mouth. In this photograph of George, aged 9 months, he has played with the plug for nearly 10 minutes. He has become so involved and engrossed he was unaware of the camera taking four or five shots of him. He played with the plug and chain with his hands, threaded it through his feet, tasted the plug end and responded in disgust, raising his arms, screwing up his face and sticking his tongue out. In this photograph he has intricately threaded the chain over his thumb and with his other thumb is sliding the chain in an upward motion.

When a treasure basket is provided in an out-of-home setting, practitioners have many responsibilities to consider, apart from selecting suitable objects, how the basket is to be used and who else will have access to it are very important.

During training sessions when discussing who a treasure basket is for, I have discovered that there are settings where a basket or container is simply put out on the floor for all the babies in the group to explore, sitters and crawlers together. This is a sure recipe for disasters of many kinds. The mobile babies will move, throw and drop inappropriate objects in other areas of the play space. It is imperative to remember that from birth to 18 months, the usual age range in a baby area, these young children's development will span from those lying on the floor, sitters, standers and cruisers.

The thought of using a treasure basket in area where sitters, standers and cruisers play together does not bear thinking about – the potential for an accident is huge. It is important that practitioners consider, debate and then ensure that only the sitters have access to the treasure basket, that they are safely positioned in an area where the crawlers, cruisers and walkers cannot get to them. Look out for:

- mobile babies reaching over and taking – dropping objects over the heads of the sitters;

*George, aged 9 months, plug play.*

- baskets which are too deep for babies to reach into;
- baskets which contain objects that are dangerous;
- baskets that tip over, causing frustration;
- baskets containing objects that are of little interest;
- baskets that contain heavy objects, such as paperweights and pebbles, being thrown by the mobile or older toddlers.

The treasure basket items are not the sorts of objects one immediately considers when thinking what to give to a young baby to play with, and responsibilities for health and safety must, as in all our efforts to provide for young babies, be considered. These areas are addressed again later in the chapter.

## Mobile babies move beyond the treasure basket

From my observations and discussions with many practitioners, there comes a time when a baby is ready to move away from the treasure basket. Once a baby becomes mobile, there is an increased risk that the contents may cause injury. Goldschmied advises that the basket is for non-mobile babies up to about 9 months. A crawling baby left unsupervised with treasure basket contents can be a danger to themselves and others. An interesting large pebble or paperweight in the treasure basket can become a lethal weapon in the hands of a crawling toddler.

During an observation (Forbes 1999c) of an 11-month-old mobile baby, Joshua, at a treasure basket, he was having a wonderful play experience with a metal flan dish of about 8 inches diameter. He was at the basket with two other younger babies, who had had less experience of the basket. They were content to explore one or two objects, but spent a lot of time watching Joshua, who confidently selected items from the basket, knowingly sorted and selected as he was familiar with some of the objects (although they were changed regularly to maintain interest).

### Joshua and the flan dish

Joshua looks again to the flan dish in front of Jessica. He picks it up, holding it higher up than previously, and drops it. He does this 16 times, he reaches for the nylon net (shower type, explored and discarded 15 minutes previously), the net is bigger than the dish, he drops the net but returns immediately to the dish. He picks up the dish and drops it again.

This observation raises important questions. Is Joshua confirming his previous first-hand experiences:

- that the dish is heavier than the net?
- that the dish is satisfyingly noisy, whereas the net makes no sound when dropped?
- that the noise of the dish changes with the differences in height and according to its landing position?

Is this the beginning of a vertical trajectory schema?

Chris Athey (1990: 37) tells us that: 'A schema, therefore, is a pattern of repeated behaviour into which experiences are assimilated and that are gradually co-ordinated. Co-ordinations lead to higher-level and more powerful schemas.' A schema is simply a pattern of play behaviour (Bruce 1997). Everyone has schemas. They are patterns of brain behaviour, which become more complex with development. Adults are very important in the development of young children's schemas, supporting and encouraging the patterns of play. Observations of babies' and young children's schemas can inform the planning for play opportunities and resources. If a young child has a schema, it will become evident, as something the child is really interested in, at home and in the setting. Discussions, not necessarily formal ones, with families might begin with 'have you noticed?', or, for example, 'Sam appears to be really interested in lining up things, this morning he was playing with the wildlife animals, lining them all up, this afternoon it was the bikes in the garden and when the wooden blocks were put out this afternoon, he made a line the length of the room and going outside'.

These sorts of conversations can help parents and families to see patterns in their children's play and begin to understand more about how play develops and how parents and practitioners can promote and extend the learning that is going on.

A trajectory schema is all about movement of objects or own body movement – jumping, throwing, moving objects in straight lines – such as lining up cars, horizontal and vertical lines and arcs – often associated with water, throwing balls and other objects to 'fly'. This is a very commonly observed schema in babies and very young children. We see them dropping things from a highchair or pram. Although nearby adults often continue the play by picking the dropped object up again, the interest for the baby is in the dropping or the downward movement of the object.

This observation of Joshua raises the question about whether the treasure basket is only appropriate for non-movers or whether a crawling baby's play can still safely be extended through it.

Here is an example where Joshua plays safely. An experienced practitioner watched Joshua, ensuring the safety of the other two babies around the basket. If he had begun to move and the possibility of hurting the other two babies occurred, then Joshua would have been moved to another area and able to continue his play. However, he was at this moment content to stay seated and explore the dish. Later on in the activity Joshua did move away from the basket with some of the objects and was content to explore near the window, where he was interested in the window cleaner and practising pulling himself up on a box.

Joshua's key person noted his delight and interest in dropping things and began to collect other objects to extend his interest. Very shortly after this observation, Joshua indicated through his own need to move around the baby room, to play and explore, and beginning, as Goldschmied observes (1989: 9), to 'pursue his own learning for himself'. Indicating to the adults that treasure basket play with a group of non-movers was no longer appropriate for him.

Objects from the baskets and others collected to support Joshua's learning were introduced in a different area in the baby room, and with the introduction of some of the objects collected for heuristic play, which we will explore further on in the book, including large tins (for dropping things in and out, making satisfying sounds) and boxes. His behaviour with other objects was recorded to see whether a schema or pattern of play (Athey 1990) was developing.

Later observations when he was nearly 2 years old show Joshua displaying a very strong interest in horizontal trajectory, lining cars up on bookcases and watching them drop off the ends. In his play he lines vehicles up on anything above the ground, indoor and out, as high as he can reach, sometimes needing a stool to help him. The nursery practitioner ensures that his play behaviour is encouraged and supported. This demonstrates the importance of early years practitioners observing, communicating, reflecting and sharing their observations. 'Observe, support, extend' Bruce (1987: 65) tells us. This applies to the youngest as well as older children. Blakemore (1998) argues, 'Babies are equipped with an inquisitive brain constructed to deal with what is around at the present.'

## Key points from this chapter ■

- Babies need 'warm-up' time at the basket, as they play. They need to gaze, feel the space and begin the exploring;
- The babies returned to the same familiar objects every time, before exploring and playing with other items in the basket – Harry, the paintbrush; Alice, metal cups; and Cerys, the cork block;
- Babies new to the nursery setting will especially need an adult to support a new activity so they can begin to play;
- Nursery planning must take into account warm-up time and the possibilities of lengthy exploration;
- A familiar room or space is desirable;
- The key person, or most important person for the babies, should sit closely, ready to support and use the time for observation;
- Three is the maximum number of babies to explore the objects comfortably and having access to a wide range of objects;
- Babies can play alone and enjoy the basket and can explore without distraction;
- Practitioners should keep the same objects in the basket for at least four sessions before changing the selection;
- Babies have favourite and familiar objects. Practitioners must respect the need for them to have these kept in the basket.

# 7

# HOW ADULTS CAN HELP TREASURE BASKET PLAY

Through the treasure basket babies can be given opportunities to play, manipulate and discover objects at their own pace and, with a basket full of at least 80 objects, to make their own choices. As the play develops, the adult role changes to that of 'indirect help', extending the babies' play and learning as Millie, Joshua's key person, did, finding similar items for him to explore. The practitioner ensures that the familiar objects are offered in a different context, thus an understanding of the babies' individual developmental needs is thoughtfully delivered.

## Offering indirect locomotive support to babies playing with the treasure basket

According to Goldschmied, the adult's role is to sit close to the baby at a treasure basket, offering emotional security and reassurance, giving facial and other body movements to indicate their presence and care, as a baby explores unfamiliar objects. During the research study, through observing Alice, I recognized how essential and powerful a sympathetic and understanding adult is. I observed the nursery practitioners strongly supporting babies' emotional needs. During discussions, they told me 'they just did it'. These practitioners were so in tune with the babies in their care they 'just did it because that was what the babies needed to be able to play'. Sitting near to the treasure basket is also an opportune time for the practitioner to be jotting down observations. Such recording will enable them to find out what else the baby shows interest in, as with Joshua:

- whether any schema or patterns of play are emerging;
- how groups of babies interact;
- which objects are explored and played with;
- to what extent and how.

## The challenge of offering play with treasure baskets

Goldschmied produced a video in 1987 with the National Children's Bureau and Islington Social Services, titled 'Infants at Work'. Part of the video was filmed in Goldschmied's home and the babies appear familiar with both their surroundings and the basket. One of the babies' mothers was also present.

The information accompanying the video addresses important questions for trainers and observers, in home and group-care situations, although it lacks detail on some of the issues. Experience of watching and working with some practitioners who have had little training on the treasure basket has raised concerns for me. There is sometimes a lack of awareness of health and safety issues. Little consideration seems to have been given to the presentation of the basket, and no thought to the space and environment.

Some of the baskets I have seen contain inappropriate contents, looking more like a sale basket from a kitchen department with collections comprising only of large, long kitchen utensils. During our discussions, Goldschmied expressed her concerns about inappropriate baskets, both in terms of use and contents. The items selected for a basket need to match the physical needs of the babies developing play, items that fit into fists, can be waved around safely, rather than so long that they touch the other babies at the basket.

## Observing babies using treasure baskets

I spent some weeks observing a group of babies playing at a treasure basket, and considered the implications of the observations for practitioners and families.

The observations began when I introduced my own treasure basket to three babies who had not yet experienced one. Through observations, I wanted to find out:

- more about the importance of the environment;
- how important the key person's role is;
- the implications for how, when and where the practitioner introduced the basket;

- whether the babies would return to familiar objects;
- how long they would play at the basket;
- how they played with the basket and the objects;
- what were the signals for 'had enough';
- what play behaviour babies showed.

I used a camcorder to record the babies at the basket once a week for four weeks. I also observed without the camera and used notes from the nursery practitioners' recording of the babies at play. I wanted to track a group of babies without prior experience of the treasure basket, to find out more about *what I thought I knew about babies' play* at the basket.

## The babies

Harry started nursery in January 2000. He was 7.2 months old when I started the video diary. He attends nursery three mornings each week.

Cerys started nursery in November 1999. She was 10.2 months old when I started the video diary. She attends nursery three full days each week.

Alice started nursery in February 2000. She was 7 months old when I started the video diary. She attends nursery three full days each week.

## Beginning the observations

The purpose of the video diary was to follow a group of babies' play experiences at the basket, to look at how they played, how they interacted, what objects they selected. I also wanted to see if they returned to any specific objects. I deliberately set out to avoid analysing their behaviour in terms of it being at any particular 'stage', as I did not want to influence or stereotype my thinking or use narrow developmental milestone descriptors. Nor was I looking for any specific skills related to stages of development. I simply wanted to see what they did, and whether this would support the change or development of current practice and thinking.

I hoped to use the video:

- as a tool to stimulate discussion with practitioners and parents;
- to observe and respond to babies' behaviour;
- to identify the considerations when introducing the basket;

- to inform future practice;
- to inform planning for encouraging and extending individual babies' play;
- to extend basket play using a range of theories which fit together with logical coherence.

In order to assess how absorbed or involved the babies became during the sessions, I used the Leuven Involvement Scale for Young Children (Laevers et al. (1997). Laevers identified a list of signals and levels of involvement up to a five-point scale. The signals are:

- concentration
- energy
- complexity and creativity
- facial expression and posture
- persistence
- precision
- reaction time
- language
- satisfaction

The description of the signals can be used to help practitioners build a picture of the child, through trying to establish how the child really feels and how involved they really are. They help the practitioner to make a judgement about the child's involvement and are not rated.

Pascal and Bertram (1996) consider that involvement cannot take place unless the emotional needs and the wellbeing of both children and practitioner are supported and addressed. This is a view shared by many early years specialists, especially those concerned with children under 3 (Selleck and Griffin 1996; Goldschmied and Jackson 1994; Elfer 1996; Manning-Morton and Thorp 2003).

'Involvement' and 'engagement' are fundamental. Babies need adults to engage with them. An engaging adult will involve a baby, and when there is a baby in the room, everyone knows, because they are so dependent on adults. They will try to engage through initiating conversation, eye pointing and vocalizing. The level of involvement signalled by a baby will depend on the relationship with the adult, whether their cues are read and interpreted or elicit a reaction.

Babies have a very strong survival motive to engage with adults. The *English Birth to Three Matters Framework* (2002) talks about a healthy child, where babies are recognized as being special and need to feel special, the emotional wellbeing of a young baby is supported through a key person and a shared understanding between home and

**Table 7.1** *Observation chart based on Leuven Involvement Scale for Young Children (1997)*

| Level 1<br>Very little activity | Baby appears listless, activity is repetitive and passive, not challenging. Baby may appear to be 'staring into space' or thinking deeply – use the involvement signs to judge this. |
|---|---|
| Level 2<br>Activity often interrupted | Only 50% of the observed time will result in activity.<br>Moments of 'staring into space' and not concentrating.<br>Interruptions/distractions detract from baby returning to activity.<br>More interested in what is going on in baby room/surroundings than at basket. |
| Level 3<br>Mainly continuous activity | Baby busy but not intensely concentrating and still easily distracted. Facial expressions determine level of mental energy, concentration is at low level. |
| Level 4<br>Activity with more intense moments | Baby concentrating more deeply, even after distraction/interruption returns to activity. Baby really involved in activity, talking to self, perhaps sharing pleasure with nearby adults. Able to identify more of the involvement signals. |
| Level 5<br>High involvement in activity | Baby deeply involved in activity. Most of the involvement signals observed. Must show 'concentration, creativity, energy, persistence and complexity'. |

setting. All the aspects of the *Framework* (2002) bring together the need for wellbeing and involvement. Recognition of babies needing close, secure relationships where they can express their feelings is essential. The *Framework* also describes babies beginning to connect with objects, and a wider group of people, making connections, and being creative and imaginative. The treasure basket responds to all these, providing opportunities for movement and sensory play and exploration, where babies can use their bodies to recreate experiences and begin to make sense and respond to the experiences of their play.

## *Week 1*

Alice had only been attending the nursery for 10 days and was still settling in. Harry and Alice were introduced to the basket in another area of the nursery, not their home base. The room was arranged to allow for camera space and they sat on the floor beside the basket. Harry had played at the nursery treasure basket on several occasions, but Alice had not.

I had chosen to film in my office, as I wanted there to be as little distraction as possible. This proved to be interesting in relation to the emotional support needed by Harry, Alice and Cerys. Sarah (the key person for all three babies) was seated to the left of the babies. Cerys joined Alice and Harry for the last 15 minutes of filming. The babies were in different surroundings, faced with two new objects (including the video camera). Although they recognized me as a familiar adult popping in and out of their home base, I had not taken any part in familiar rituals such as nappy changing and feeding. I had only been involved in their play when adults who were more familiar were with them. Now I was behind the camera and another possible source of distraction. The babies stayed at the basket for 30 minutes in total for this session. Alice was lifted away from the basket as soon as we felt she was struggling. However, after a few minutes out with Sarah she returned to the basket.

### *Learning from observations*

Close relationships are important for babies, particularly in the nursery. Elfer (1996) suggests that it is difficult to sustain 'close and responsive' relationships unless there is a culture that supports and reflects the emotional dimension of practice. In this section, Sarah is the anchor for Alice in a new situation. Alice is lifted away from the basket twice during the 30 minutes as soon as her distress and struggle with a new situation become too much for her and us. Alice was not confident in this situation, easily crying and anxious. However, the reassurance from Sarah was enough to support Alice to return to the basket quite soon. When the three babies are at the basket together, Alice appeared more relaxed and connected with the activity again by becoming involved with a piece of loofah. She also explored the texture of the woven floor mat. All the babies at some point played with the floor mat, a specially selected woven wicker mat, used only to put the treasure basket on. The importance of the emotional content of Alice's experience with the basket and with the adult she loves was constantly recognized and addressed. Alice also looked at Harry several times. He settled to the basket readily, vocalizing towards the camera and Sarah several times. Alice touched the basket after Harry had rummaged. She seemed to be reassured by Harry's actions and contentment. I filmed 30 minutes of the first session: Harry played for 45 minutes, Alice approximately 25 minutes and Cerys 15 minutes.

### Persistent play

Harry demonstrated persistence; he attempted to pick up the metal cup as it slid across the mat. Using a fine pincer grip and almost doubled over, he pushed the cup along the carpet and eventually picked it up. Harry was easily distracted during this session, the doorbell rang and he looked to the window as he heard people passing by outside. He vocalized to himself and to both adults present. The signals Harry demonstrated during this session were concentration, facial expression and posture, language and satisfaction. I think he was working at Level 3 of the Leuven Involvement Scale. This means he was fairly involved (see Table 7.1). Alice was easily distracted and took longer to settle and explore the contents. Several times, she brushed the top of the basket. I think Alice was working at Level 2, her language signals tell us she was less sure. Her facial expressions and posture indicated helplessness and the need for reassurance from her anchor adult. Cerys settled quickly to the basket, and she vocalized quietly as she explored the basket and objects.

| Objects selected and played with | | |
|---|---|---|
| **Alice** | **Harry** | **Cerys** |
| Loofah | Paintbrush | Wooden block |
| Metal cup | Pine cone | Nail brush |
| Floor mat | Small wicker mat | Small cork |
| Shoe brush | Wooden block | Floor mat |
| Honey dipper | Large shell | |
| | Loofah | |
| | Small cork | |
| | Metal cups | |
| | Linked metal spoons | |
| | Honey dipper | |

## Week 2

Alice and Cerys spent approximately 30 minutes together at the basket during the morning. I observed their play but did not film them. Harry was absent from nursery. Later, in one of the baby rooms, where she was in a familiar environment, I filmed Cerys at the basket for 15 minutes. Sarah was also present.

*Video diary: Cerys playing on her own*

Cerys scanned the basket and vocalized. She showed interest in the cork block and played with it for some time. She flicked the cork block out of reach. During this session, Cerys played with the sounds of the bottle and the shell. She mouthed both ends of the bottle, displaying delight in the sound produced at the neck of the bottle. Cerys' attention returned to the cork block on several occasions, trying to move it nearer. She succeeded in up-ending the block and grasping it again.

She appeared very interested in sounds, playing for several minutes with the bottle in the bowl of the large shell, moving her head and listening. Then she vocalized, singing sometimes quite loudly. Her pleasure in the sounds appeared to be transferred to her own voice. Cerys found the foot roller. Her whole body enjoyed the experience as she stretched her arms vertically above her head, and then horizontally in front of her. Her legs stretched and her toes curled over the roller. She shared her pleasure of the foot roller with the watching adult, looking at them, looking to the roller and back to the adult. Cerys then explored the metal cups. She dropped the green bottle out of reach, and then looked to the adult, with her right thumb in her mouth, twisting the small metal cup in her other hand, in a waving motion at the adult. Her vocalization became quieter, softer. Had she just caught her reflection in the flat end of the cup? It seemed so. For the next two minutes Cerys persisted at the two metal cups caught on the floor between her legs. She implemented several strategies, raising her voice, pushing and pulling the objects, banging the side of the basket. Her vocalization changed, with longer, pronounced, 'ayeeee, ayeee' sounds and a higher pitch. She looked up several times in the direction of the adults. When she eventually picked up the metal cup, her pleasure in her success was obvious and was shared with the adults.

*Learning from observations*

Cerys appeared content alone at the basket, though she looked at the adults present on several occasions, seeking reassurance, checking out what was happening around her, and sharing her pleasure with the objects. Discussion with the nursery practitioner led to the information that Cerys was 'into exploring sounds now'. This certainly seemed to be confirmed by her play at the basket. Having established that the green bottle produced a noise when she mouthed it, she played with the bottle for a long period, mouthing it and exploring it to the full. She put both ends into her mouth, but soon discovered which end the sounds came from and repeatedly played with both ends to keep checking out and reaffirm her understanding of what this object was. Cerys was deepening her understanding of cause and effect, when her own body was part of the cause. Cerys also explored other sounds produced by banging the bottle onto the large shell. Cerys used her senses to the full, including what Goldschmied calls the 'sixth sense', that of bodily movement or kinaesthesia, the linking of movement and learning.

Goddard Blythe's (1998) work has shown how vital physical play experience is to learning and play. She suggests that the development of modern baby equipment has resulted in young babies spending less time on the floor. She confirms that children learn best when they relate physically and emotionally to new material.

It would have been easy for an adult to intervene and give Cerys the metal cups, but I was interested to see for how long she would persist. Too often adults intervene and prevent babies from succeeding. Here Cerys was delighted with her success. Cerys is concentrating during this session but can be distracted. She is energetic in her explorations, vocalizing loudly and often. Cerys is signalling her complexity and creativity and persistence (during the attempts to pick up the metal pots), language and satisfaction are demonstrated. I think Cerys was working at Level 3 as some of the signals for involvement were observed, but not all and not consistently.

| Objects selected and played with | | | |
|---|---|---|---|
| Cork block | Loofah | Large shell | Roller |
| 2 metal pots | Paintbrush | Green bottle | Pine cone |

## *Week 3*

### *Planning never (or rarely) goes to plan*

During week 3, Cerys was absent from nursery. Harry and Alice were seated at the treasure basket in one of the two baby rooms, a familiar room but not their home base. At 12.30 both babies had had lunch, Harry goes home at 1pm, and Alice spends a full day at nursery. Sarah sat alongside Alice out of camera shot. Alice appears 'not herself', but we were unable to identify a cause.

### *Harry and Alice at the basket*

Harry is seated first; he reached straight for the paintbrush. Holding the paintbrush in his right hand, he used his toes to explore the side of the basket. He used a raking movement with the paintbrush across the top of the basket in an attempt to move the pine cone nearer. His whole body moved, he used his thigh to lean against the basket for increased stability. He stopped and looked at the pine cone. Using the paintbrush in his right hand, he pulled the brush across the top of the basket. He then balanced the paintbrush across the rim of the basket and with the bristles in his right hand, rummaged in the basket with his left. He then put the handle of the brush upright on the floor as a support, leant on it and rummaged in the basket with his left hand. His toes grasped the side of the basket. Harry was using his body and the objects as tools to support his play.

Harry is becoming increasingly mobile. He raised himself onto his haunches and leans precariously at times. Alice joined Harry and there was acknowledgement of her arrival. Alice reached straight for the metal cup. Harry was aware of the mirror on the wall behind him, and glanced over his shoulder at his and Alice's reflection, whilst waving the brush. Alice reached for another metal cup, cried, and was reassured by Sarah, she banged two cups together, vocalized almost a cry, Harry looks over with a bemused expression. Harry and Alice watched each other whilst interacting with the cups; Harry was still watching and almost lost his balance. He lunged across the basket with the paintbrush, the pine cone moved, he stopped and looked. Then he used the paintbrush as a rake to move the pine cone. Alice was still banging cups, she made a quiet cry and Harry mouthed silently, he might have been imitating her facial expression. Harry had made a little heap of objects around himself.

Harry watched Alice playing with the linked spoons, jangling the set; he slid his upturned metal pot onto the carpet, leaning right over to move it along. He was distracted by her short cry. Alice is reassured again by Sarah, this time by some gentle stroking of Alice's back. She leant into the basket and stroked the shoe brush, then cried and turned away. Alice was then distracted by whistling, the window cleaner was outside; Harry looked at Alice and then followed her gaze to the window. Harry enjoyed the large shell in between his legs, opening and closing them and scratching the shiny surface with his fingers. He then continued to gently rummage in the basket. He had moved slightly away from the side of the basket and was sitting / leaning precariously. Kirsten, Harry's mum, arrived whilst we were filming and in his delight at hearing her voice, he completely over balanced and began to cry a little. We signalled to Kirsten that it was alright to come over – we could see she wanted to and Harry needed her – she picked Harry up, and he immediately stopped crying and smiled broadly.

### Learning from observations

Alice still appeared unsettled at the basket; she needed reassurance from Sarah and only played with objects fleetingly. She was easily distracted and at times distracted Harry. There was definite interaction between the two and Harry appeared to show concern for Alice's distress. Sarah tuned in to Alice's needs, and at my suggestion slid her arm across and stroked her back. This had immediate effect. I wanted to see if Alice needed more than the reassuring glances that Goldschmied suggests. I did not want to take Alice away from the basket, but to support her with her struggles.

During discussions, the practitioners reported that they seemed to pick Alice up constantly. As she was still settling into the nursery, getting to know Sarah and the team, it was a difficult time for her. She needed reassurance and to know that she would be supported through cuddles and talk from the new adults. The team agreed to be consistent with Alice, not to immediately pick her up but to sit and talk with her, touch her, sit close to her on the floor, playing together. The length of time needed for babies to develop close relationships and become comfortable with a new environment varies. There are no set rules and every baby will be different and have different needs, which the practitioners need to identify and respond to.

Harry's explorations for the first three minutes were very intense. Harry manipulated the paintbrush using a raking motion; perhaps this was the beginning of using objects as tools. He was beginning to play and seemed to be thinking and working out how objects can influence each other and how the brush caused the pine cone to wobble (but not enough to make it move towards him). Practitioners will give Harry the opportunity to practise this and as his language develops to include 'uh oh', so will his ability to use objects as tools. He had become more mobile in a week and almost toppled over several times in this session. Harry's first object was the paintbrush again. He looked over to Alice on several occasions and appeared to show concern for her distress. Babies can feel 'sad for each other' (Dunn 1998) and Harry's expression as he looked at Alice appeared sad.

Alice and Harry were at Level 2, as the activity was often inter-rupted and only half of the observation time was spent concentrating on the basket contents.

| Objects selected and played with | |
| --- | --- |
| **Alice** | **Harry** |
| Metal pans<br>Linked spoons | Paintbrush<br>Large shell<br>Metal pans |

## Week 4

### Babies playing together

All three babies were already playing at the treasure basket in the baby room for 15 minutes before I began filming. The level of play immediately seemed different, it was more intense and the periods of concentration on objects were longer. The interaction and interplay between all three babies was more sustained. Harry selected the paintbrush immediately, Cerys the cork block and Alice the metal cups.

Harry leant over to take a cup from Alice, she was distracted and Harry took the cup. Alice looked as if she was about to protest but did not. She carried on with the other cup. Harry then took the other cup when Alice was distracted. She appeared to protest quietly, but watched Cerys to her side and slightly behind her, waving the linked spoons noisily. Harry was beginning to move away from the side of the basket. Alice rummaged and reached the shoe brush, bringing it out using both hands. Cerys was using the wall, playing with the objects, banging the cup and linked spoons on it. Alice took the red pot from the basket using both her hands and mouthed it. The narrow end of the pot slid, and Alice showed surprise, as she looked at the two parts. With one part in her hand she used two hands to pick up the other part and then bang them together. Alice put her hand inside the pot and took it to her mouth.

Cerys was playing noisily, banging objects together on the wall and the wooden skirting board. She was also using her mouth. Harry moved away from the basket, shuffling on his bottom, he had created a heap of objects and out of camera shot was exploring them. He looked at his reflection in the upturned metal pot on the floor. He was chatting to himself.

Alice played with the plug and chain, using her mouth, feet and hands. She played with this for some time, beginning to play for a sustained period. She dropped the plug into her lap and found the blue stopper and, mouthing it, felt the cool acrylic with her hands; she returned to the plug, picked it up and pulled the plug chain taut, showing surprise and dropping the plug. Alice then selected the curtain ring and banged the ring and stopper together. Harry found one half of the red pot and rolled it on the carpet using the palm of his hand. He watched Cerys playing with the plug and took it from her. He spent several minutes playing. Alice then selected the large shell and the green bottle to play with.

## Learning from observations

Alice, Harry and Cerys were at the basket for 1 hour 15 minutes. They played independently of each other but watched each other, sometimes quite intently. Many objects were explored, and it was difficult to keep track. Alice experienced something 'inside' and hidden becoming 'outside', and the beginnings of mathematics when the red pot divided in her hands. She showed surprise and then played with both parts. As she put her hand inside the pot, I think Alice was exploring 'containment or enveloping', an early schema described by Athey (1990: 149), or 'inside', as attributed to Bower by Athey.

This was a complex experience for Alice; she was on the edge of complex and creative skills. It would be interesting to give Alice other objects that divide or that she could fit her hand into. Harry was quite a competent bottom-shuffler by now and played with a selection of objects away from Alice and Cerys. His posture indicated his level of concentration and occasionally he glanced over to the others. He moved, using his haunches to shuffle him back to the basket to find more objects and to watch the others. Alice was far more settled and confident. She did not protest when Harry took a cup from her, instead she chose another object. Alice was concentrating for long periods on objects, mouthing, stroking, banging, patting, and she used her toes as an extension of her senses to feel the chain.

I think Alice and Harry were at Level 5. During the session I observed concentration, energy, complexity and creativity, persistence and precision. Language consisted of vocalizing to themselves, to each other and the watching adults. Cerys was working at Level 4; she had some intense moments but was still distracted often by the sounds she was creating and playing with. She was very energetic in her play and exploration of sounds, making different sounds with objects, quite noisy at times, and also making her own sounds.

| Objects selected and played with | | |
|---|---|---|
| **Harry** | **Alice** | **Cerys** |
| Paintbrush | Metal cups | Cork block |
| Metal cups | Cork block | Linked spoons |
| Lemon squeezer | Shoe brush | Metal cup |
| Spectacle case | Red pot | Cork block |
| Patty tin | Foot roller | Horn ring |
| Plug and chain | Plug and chain | Marmite jar |
| Large shell | Acrylic stopper | Glass jar |
| Red pot | Large shell | Egg cup |
| Large cork block | Pine cone | Small tin |
| | Small green bottle | Honey dipper |
| | Wooden curtain ring | Small shell |
| | | Large shell |
| | | Red pot |

## Observing each week records a world of play

The video of the babies as they play has shown how important the environment is, the role of the sensitive and 'tuned in' adult, and the value of observation. It has also shown that babies do not need an adult to introduce objects to them. Babies, given a variety of interesting objects, will choose for themselves which they want to explore. They also decide for how long and how to explore. The longest time spent at the basket was 1 hour 15 minutes, without interruptions or signals for 'had enough'. This has implications for planning in the nursery. The 'when' and 'how' to use a treasure basket both have to be considered before putting out the basket and the babies around it.

## Babies need 'warm-up time'

One of the key learning points from the observations of Harry, Cerys and Alice is about warm-up time. Practitioners planning for treasure basket play sessions will have to consider the length of time needed for settling and 'rummaging'. The babies needed warm-up time to become reacquainted with the basket.

The first session demonstrated clearly how all the babies needed a long time to familiarize themselves with the basket and the surroundings. The first morning's recording in an unknown room was not the ideal place. Babies and children were frequent visitors to my office, but only to say hello, not to stay! The video clearly shows how Alice needed encouragement and support. She settled to play with the contents but needed to come away from the basket for an occasional cuddle. The first session lasted for 45 minutes, although I did not film for that time. The babies spent longer at the basket when there were three of them.

During Week 2 Cerys was filmed alone, although she explored the basket fully and did not signal 'had enough' for 30 minutes. I thought she interacted with the adults more during this session.

By the fourth week, the play had changed considerably. The babies were completely involved in the objects, there was much inter-play and the basket contents were fully explored, all over the floor.

The nursery needs to be planned to allow the babies a safe space, where an adult can sit near them and other mobile children cannot. Babies need space to play and explore and concentrate securely, without interruption from other 'crawling invaders', as one practitioner commented.

## Debating the lack of play

Just as babies and children learn through first-hand rich experiences, practitioners also benefit from hands-on experience of a well-stocked treasure basket, and support from an experienced user of the basket.

Practitioners made these comments during and following training sessions on the treasure basket and the needs of children under 3:

> No wonder our babies don't play much with our treasure basket, it isn't really a treasure basket at all, we haven't got half as many things in ours.

We have organized a parents' evening following our treasure basket training and want to get them involved in collecting for the basket and understanding why we want a really lovely basket and what their babies will learn.

## Learning about treasure

Everyone who is going to use the basket needs to have a clear understanding of the treasure basket principles. Parents appreciate being involved in learning about and contributing to the basket and how it supports their children's play and learning.

Practitioners will need to consider the following when planning for introducing a treasure basket:

Why...

- are you offering babies a treasure basket?
- it just seems like a collection of junk...

Who...

- is going to be responsible for the basket?
- will check all the items for appropriateness and safety?
- will clean the objects after every use?

How...

- will you offer it to the babies – think about the safe space issue, and propping babies comfortably if they are not able to sit unsupported?
- will you ensure your basket reflects the home experiences of all your babies?
- will you support practitioners and parents who are not sure about the basket?
- will you record your observations of babies play and learning?

What...

- is the role of the adult at the basket, and do all the practitioners understand how to apply it?
- are you going to put in your basket?
- will you see as babies begin to play?

When...

- are you going to start collecting items?
- are you going to train the practitioners to use the basket safely?

## Parents learning about their baby's play    ■

I was invited to join a parents' evening in a new setting to introduce the treasure basket to a group of parents, some of whom were pregnant. I used sections of 'Infants at Work' (1987), the National Children's Bureau video, and brought along my own treasure basket.

I began the evening by handing each adult (including the nursery practitioner), a commercial baby toy or part of a toy, made from plastic. I suggested to them that I would leave them to 'play' for a while, and proposed that they consider how their babies would tackle the toys, through smelling, mouthing and touching. Immediately, one adult requested whether she 'could have something else' to go with her plastic ball.

The group was asked to imagine that they had to 'play' for 20 minutes, they were not allowed to exchange or share their toys, imitating as closely as possible the play experience of their young babies. The adult play did not last for many minutes and promoted interesting dialogue: 'I've done everything', 'I have had enough of this', and 'I think I am learning to crawl very quickly'.

The group of parents was then given an object from the treasure basket and asked to 'play' with it. Much more time was spent on this, with the group discussing amongst themselves the properties of their object. The discussion then focused on the objects, drawing comparisons with the plastic experience, with questions and observations from everyone in the group:

- What was it?
- What was it made of?
- What did it feel like?
- Did it smell?
- What was it like when you mouthed the object, the taste and texture in your mouth?
- Was it heavy, light?
- Could you squeeze it, knead it and/or bang it?
- Did it move when you put it on the floor?
- Could you eat/taste it? (I have an orange, lemon and lime in my basket)

- How did the play experience with the object from the treasure basket compare with that of the plastic toy?
- Which did you prefer?

The group then watched some clips of 'Infants at Work' (1987) followed by a discussion of the objects featured in the video, the purpose of the basket and the potential for the play and learning experience. Several parents raised concerns over the clip showing the baby chewing the bottlebrush, because it was made of twisted wire with a bristle end. The clip shows a baby chewing and waving it vigorously. Although Goldschmied reassures the listener with the comments that the baby is not sufficiently coordinated to poke any of the other babies seated near him or himself, the group raised several questions. This revives the questions discussed earlier in relation to the glass bottle given to me by Goldschmied.

Debate has to take place about objects (not only those from the treasure basket but those offered in other play contexts) of and for play and their contribution to the beginnings of play. The group was reassured that a bottlebrush was not included in either my basket or that of their setting.

The group was fascinated by the treasure basket and rummaged through it as if it were a bargain box on a market stall. I introduced to them the idea of collections and how babies like to explore all the things we try to keep out of their reach. We talked about how many adults have 'collections'. By carefully selecting the contents, the basket can become a link between nursery, home and the community, with the contents reflecting the local environment.

After watching the video, the group discussed the length of time babies had spent exploring and concentrating, 'sitting that long really engrossed'. I explained how the babies were making choices, selecting, discarding and staying with one or more objects for some time. Looking at the clips, parents were able to identify some of these actions.

The evening had begun with concerns over some of the objects, but ended with a group of parents understanding far more about the treasure basket and their babies' play and learning experiences. Those who had babies in the nursery were reassured on:

- matters of hygiene;
- safety and safe selection of objects;
- the purpose of the basket.

Feedback from this group was very positive. If each parent who attended chats to just one other parent about the evening then the setting will have made positive moves towards developing partnership with their parents and encouraging families to become part of their very young children's play and learning.

It is important that early years settings consider the lifestyle and working patterns of their families. Offering sessions such as the treasure basket evening that meet and fit with their home and work patterns is important. If families are to be seen by early years practitioners as partners in, rather than consumers of, children's services, they must be able to attend and inform meetings. Families will then really become part of a collaborative relationship, contributing to the service and being active in decision-making, as were the small group of parents I met with.

There had been a specific request concerning omission of some of the items suggested for treasure basket play that were respected and acknowledged. This might be viewed by some as a small or even insignificant contribution to the beginning of babies' play, but it is a vital one, to encourage families to be active partners, and knowledgeable about the provision and practice leading to their babies' play.

## Key points from this chapter

- The practitioner's role is about facilitating and supporting play experiences at the treasure basket, not directing;
- Practitioners will need to become close observers, attuned to babies' signals so that they are responsive to their play and emotional needs around the basket;
- The practitioner will need to safely select and regularly check objects to maintain the health and safety of the babies and the basket;
- The objects selected for a treasure basket must match the physical needs of the babies developing and changing play;
- An exciting, interesting basket will offer babies opportunities for long periods of involvement and concentration;
- Parents and practitioners will need to begin to debate the objects offered and share the learning about babies' play at the basket;
- Parents appreciate knowing about and want to be involved in their babies' play and learning at the basket.

# 8

# MOVING INTO HEURISTIC PLAY

Collections and collectors of objects tend to draw adults and children alike. Think of the people you know who adorn their cars or bedrooms with cushions, dolls, teddies, colleagues who prop little groups of soft toys near or on their computer (I am staring at a grinning bumble bee). For some it will be toys, others, shells, pebbles, miniature pots and bottles.

Practitioners working creatively with older children will know how useful collections like these can be for adding to the children's interest. Useful tools for learning using first-hand, real experiences can be gathered by asking children to bring in toys such as a teddy for a project on bears or objects to add to the collection and using this as a springboard for learning. For example, a collection of teddies could encourage a child to tell me about:

- where the teddies come from;
- their names;
- what they like to do;
- where have the teddies travelled;
- which is the oldest/youngest teddy;
- how many teddies there are in the collection;
- which are the biggest/smallest;
- how many are wearing waistcoats/bow ties/skirts;
- the clothes they are wearing.

Younger children too can be introduced to the notion of collections. Having already experienced a wonderful treasure basket, babies will revel in the imagination and creativity of the practitioners as they extend experiences with a new set of objects. The key element is to build on the experiences and support the things that the baby is interested in. As the babies become more mobile, they will have begun to explore the resources that make up the environment, making it clear what they are interested in.

## Treasuring and learning from play experiences ■

Just as the practitioners set up areas to stimulate and extend Joshua's interest and play pattern, this can be done for groups of babies to experience beginning to play in small groups. The opportunity for playing and communicating, beginnings of sociable communication, are available.

There are many debates to be had about the play experiences that happen at the treasure basket. Harry at 7.3 months, when he first used the paintbrush accidentally as a 'rake' to reach the pine cone and then later repeated the action, was demonstrating assimilation and accommodation, using what he already knew in a different way. The treasure basket can provide early mathematical experiences, as for Alice and the dividing pot.

Gopnik et al. (1999: 144) conclude that since videotape technology became more readily available, and more women have become scientists and more male scientists have looked after young babies, 'we began to pay more real attention to babies'. Parents and primary carers have to be part of this learning process (Athey 1990; Whalley 2001) sharing their first-hand knowledge and contributing to, initiating and organizing discussions concerned with their children. As children become more skilled, they too can be part of the research process, telling us what we need to know about their needs, likes, interests and how they learn best. Babies need us to be really responsive observers, able to understand and interpret as they tell us and show us with very little spoken language what they are interested in and what they are not.

## Re-using treasures ■

Babies I have observed at the treasure basket have shown that the more complex the object they are given to explore, the more sustained and involved their play and learning becomes. Experiences introduced to extend the babies' play using observations from the treasure basket are essential.

The following photographs show Alice and Cerys using familiar objects in a different context.

*Recycled and re-used familiar play objects.*

Cerys is playing with the familiar curtain rings. With a curtain pole end the play is changed. The cubby holes store a range of familiar and new treasures that the babies safely select from and can begin to play with in a new or different way.

Alice and Cerys playing with Sarah, both are physically and emotionally close to her in this shot. Alice had been taking all the beanbags from the cubby holes of the locker and giving them to Sarah and then taking them back from her. Her repeated play pattern of giving and taking included the corks and shells from a basket. Cerys had been enjoying the curtain rings and pole ends, this time she had had her finger in the bottom of the pole end and had been attempting to roll the pole end on the flat wooden surface. She was also playing with the sounds from these objects, repeatedly banging them onto the locker or banging them together like a pair of cymbals.

*Playing with and sharing significant others.*

## Collecting treasure

Small collections of objects from the treasure basket can be offered to babies once they become mobile. All the health and safety considerations for the treasure basket apply with heuristic play objects. Set up areas with a large tin or container and a collection of curtain rings or corks which might have been played with in the basket. Babies and young children delight in fitting things on to something else with their developing hand–eye coordination skills, so they will become really involved in this. Mug trees are useful resources to use for this type of play activity. Collect a variety of things that will hang on the tree, for example:

- a range of curtain hooks – metal, wooden, different sizes;
- bracelets – plastic, wooden, metal;
- large chain link – take care of the weight – have three or four links safely linked. Some chain link is plastic coated – use both.

Roll holders meant for kitchen towels are perfect early stacking playthings. These can be cut to a size that makes them ideal for seated babies. Ensure they are cut and rounded off safely. For older, mobile children these can be left at full size, allowing for any number of objects to be stacked over the ring.

## Heuristic play ▪

'Heuristic play with objects' was developed and put into practice by Goldschmied following work with practitioners in Europe and the UK. It is defined as 'offering an activity for a group of children, for a defined period of time in a controlled environment, a large number of different kinds of objects and receptacles with which they play freely without adult intervention' (Goldschmied and Jackson 1994: 118).

Heuristic play is an approach which offers young children between 12 and 20 months the opportunity to play with a range of objects that both satisfies and promotes their schema (play pattern) of needing to fill and empty everything in sight. By offering a heuristic play session, the practitioner is able to support the play of these young children, who are often labelled by less experienced practitioners as 'in to everything' and 'flitting from one thing to another', or dismissed as being 'toddlers who can't concentrate on anything'.

### *Making a collection*

Goldschmied (1994) offers suggestions for objects for heuristic play collections and in the National Children's Bureau video (1992). These are some of the things I have collected and used or seen used:

| *Receptacles* – think sound and size – try to have a wide variety, as the children will be dropping or putting things into them: | |
| --- | --- |
| • large tins – catering size with the tops made completely safe<br>• tins of different shapes and sizes – long thin/oval type used for Italian biscuits, formula milk tins, hexagonal biscuit tins<br>• shallower containers, baskets, cardboard boxes – shoe boxes, different sizes<br>• savoury snack tubes<br>• mug tree<br>• kitchen roll holder | • solid inner cardboard tubes with no bottom – again go for variety of sizes<br>• whisky tubes – some have metal bottoms and others cardboard – try to get both<br>• knitting cones – these are available in plastic and cardboard, ridged or smooth<br>• clear plastic drink containers with wide tops – so that the objects dropped in can be retrieved |

When collecting objects or materials for putting into the containers, think about things which will roll, fit on to the containers and fit into the containers.

| Suggestions for objects: | |
|---|---|
| • lids of all different sizes, shapes and material<br>• ping-pong balls<br>• cotton reels<br>• hair curlers, foam and plastic<br>• small knitting cones<br>• lengths of *securely linked* chain, fine to medium weights<br>• pom-poms<br>• plastic measuring scoops (from formula tins)<br>• used keys – ensure they are blunt by doing a tongue test, keep them linked together | • small foam balls<br>• shells<br>• pine cones<br>• corks – different sizes<br>• lengths of ribbon, suede, or other fabric<br>• lolly sticks or tongue depressors<br>• bracelets, curtain rings, anything which will 'fit on to'<br>• pegs – dolly type<br>• wooden door/furniture knobs<br>• very large buttons<br>• medium-sized pebbles |

Heuristic play offers the young child the opportunity to find out through first-hand experience what the objects 'will and will not do'. The practitioner needs to ensure that there are enough containers for the number of children playing and Goldschmied suggests that there needs to be a minimum of 50 objects. So a 'collection' that is individual to the setting and children will develop as families are encouraged to help suggest and source suitable objects. The practitioner's role is to:

- Set out the collection in a safe area;
- Select and check the objects for safety;
- Allow 3 to 4 containers per child;
- Use at least 15 collections of objects per group of children;
- Observe and record;
- Promote and encourage the play and learning.

For many young children sifting through a pile of objects heaped together attractively in the room will be satisfying enough.

### Setting out the play area

- Ensure that the space is large enough and does not interfere with other play activities. Ideally another room or a cordoned-off area is best.
- Set the containers out around the space with a collection of objects near them.
- Bring the children into the play space.

By setting out an area specifically, the message to the children is that this is something different, with new and exciting materials. They will probably begin to play by inspecting the set-up, this in itself is an interesting aspect of the play and if you are introducing this sort of play to a new group of children, allow them the time to move around the room and observe as they inspect the attractive collections of objects, inspect the containers – 'what is in here then?' and 'what's this for?' They need to see what is on offer before they can begin to play. Some practitioners heap similar objects together, others offer heaps of combined objects. There are no rules, apart from those of safety. For young children new to heuristic play, having the same objects heaped together might be more helpful, as the initial play will be about examining, with children talking about 'what are all these wonderful things?'.

One group of toddlers new to heuristic play played in a separate room from their normal play space for nearly 45 minutes. A television crew filming an aspect of toddlers' play wanted to see some heuristic play. After 15 minutes of engrossed, almost silent play, the cameraman whispered – because none of us felt we could talk in anything but hushed tones, so engrossed and involved were these toddlers – 'how long will they play for, can you tell me when the session is over, I cannot believe how busy these little children are'.

### *Beginning to play with collections*

The play of these young children observed during heuristic play sessions has, as already mentioned, been observed to be deeply involved and absorbed. They need very little encouragement from the practitioner, who can be seated close by, just as for the treasure basket, to offer reassurance or explanation as appropriate, but not to direct the play. Some children will need some encouragement, a look that says 'yes, you can stack the tins like that' or reassurance if the noise from the objects hitting the bottom of a container has startled a child. By offering a range of containers and an appropriate number, there is usually very little conflict between these young children, who are not yet ready to share or take turns.

During one heuristic play session I observed, Oliver, aged 15 months, played with a collection of pegs. He was slightly older than the rest of the toddlers and had played with some of the collection previously. Several toddlers gathered round his space, as Oliver was dropping objects methodically into the large tin. One of the other toddlers picked up an object, dropped it in and waited. Oliver did the same, and so this continued round the tin as Oliver allowed the other three toddlers to drop objects into the tin. The other toddlers then moved off and Oliver remained with the tin, tipping everything out.

These very young children will fill, empty and sort out the objects. Full or empty containers and objects may be carried around (supporting a transporting schema). Collections will be dropped, poured and tipped into the containers and the resulting sounds played and explored. During the play the toddlers will discover that things are not always as they seem – as they play with tins, boxes, and bottomless tubes.

Tidying-up time from a heuristic play session needs to be included in the time plan. Encouraging the children to bring the objects to the adult and put them into the storage bag or container supports mathematical concepts, sorting the objects into sets and sizes. Practitioners will need to make sure they show the children the objects and then give them the language for the objects and the containers as the materials are sorted – 'Can you find the big shells please?' 'We need all the lids collected now please.' If another object is brought to the bag, other than the sort being collected, the practitioner needs to thank the child, place the object nearby and then show the child the object again and perhaps point to one on the floor, 'Thank you for the shell Sam, I'll need that later; look, Sam, over there, I need all the lids please.' An important part of play is tidying up, and this helps the child to begin to take responsibility for putting resources away in the early years setting.

## Bag and box play

Babies and young children, as we have already identified, spend a lot of time putting things in and taking things out of containers, as well as transporting or moving things around their environment. Bags and boxes can support this play. Collect and provide handbags, shopping bags, haversacks, large paper carrier bags, briefcases and any sort of bag, preferably one from the real world, that can be crammed full of bricks, sand, paper, small world animals and people, pieces of jigsaw puzzle, anything that the young child is playing with and wants to move to somewhere else! In one setting the practitioners introduced a very large cardboard box (after safety checks) that had transported an industrial washing machine to the baby room. The front flaps were open, inviting a look round. The babies gazed for a long period of time at this new visitor, the practitioner walked a large teddy into the box and then asked if he was alright inside the box. After another period of time, Frazer crawled to the box, and peered in. He then crawled slowly and hesitantly inside the box, retreating quickly, smiling and dragging teddy out. Over the afternoon the mobile babies all ventured inside the box. They were heard cooing, chatting and laughing, listening to their own voices echoing inside the box, banging and tapping on the insides and outside of the box, playing peep-bo and later when a sag bag was put inside, stories were read by the practitioner perched half in and half out of the box.

Sam (17 months) and Jack (19 months) are walking down the shared play area in an early years setting, where children can play freely in home base space or the shared space. This large shared area has been set out with sand play, painting, and a large climbing frame rearranged with the underneath space inviting home play. The upstairs of the climbing frame is the 'babies' bedrooms' with cots, cushions and books.

Sam and Jack are walking purposefully side by side, each carrying an empty bucket; they are heading towards the climbing frame, where a small group of children are playing. As I walk towards them they beam at me; 'goin' shops', Sam says, waving the bucket in his hand. I look around at another small group of children, all carrying handbags and shopping bags from the trolley near the climbing frame. Sam and Jack are clearly determined to be part of this slightly older group of children, all 2.5 years and above. By bringing their own 'bags' to the play, Sam and Jack were beginning to find out how to be part of other children's play.

The environments we offer for babies' and young children's play need to be functional, easy to use and aesthetically pleasing, for children and practitioners. Sam and Jack moved comfortably in the shared space, knowing that watchful and caring adults were close to hand if needed or sometimes to be part of the play.

The principles of heuristic play with objects (Goldschmied and Jackson 1994) can be applied to other play experiences for children up to 3. Consider the 'art' experiences observed and described by Selleck in Chapter 4; she is not alone in her observations of these inappropriate 'activities'. Gluing, sand play, gloop, paint and water play, there are many play experiences which practitioners will need to consider to ensure that they are offered to babies and toddlers to provide exciting and interesting play experiences, through consideration of place, space, resources and purpose of the experience. I observed a group of three babies, all under 1 year, playing on the

*Boxes are always good for play, supporting wobbly walkers or playing peep-bo.*

floor at individual trays of gloop. They were able to use their hands and feet, faces, bare tummies (they were only wearing nappies) to play with and experience the gloop. They sat beside the trays and used their hands, they balanced on their haunches and spread their hands across the tray, they lowered themselves into the trays, and they moved to inspect and test out each other's trays. The practitioner sat alongside these babies. She offered reassuring glances and language, ensured the space was kept safe for the babies as more and more gloop moved from trays to mat, she allowed the babies time and space to play. There was no 'end product', it was all washed away, a happy memory for the babies and some photographs and discussion to share with families about the afternoon's play.

## Key points from this chapter

- Babies will tell us what they are interested in, practitioners need to be able to respond and provide appropriate play experiences;
- Small collections of objects from the treasure basket can be offered to babies once they become mobile.
- Heuristic play offers the young child the opportunity to find out through first-hand experience what the objects 'will and will not do';
- Recycled and re-usable treasures from the real world can become part of the setting's collections;
- Collections need to reflect the developing and changing interests and mobility of young children;
- The principles of heuristic play with objects can be re-applied to other aspects of young children's play.

# 9

# TUNING IN: TALKING AND LISTENING

The strong silent type is not much good to a small child. ...
From earliest infancy children need conversation.

(Purves and Selleck 1999: 87)

This chapter is not about language development, the stages of language, or a debate as to whether language is acquired or learned. For the student wanting to read about these areas there are plenty of more eloquent and informative texts available.

'Infant' comes from the Latin 'infans', meaning 'unable to speak'. To call our babies 'infants' does not do them justice – we know that although they might not yet have the words, they certainly are able to communicate and for those babies and young children for whom oral language will always be a challenge, there are other ways of communication.

I want to start at the premise that all babies and young children come equipped to communicate; we as parents, practitioners, significant other adults simply have to think about tuning into an individual child's communication strategy, and sometimes for some babies and young children that will be more challenging than the communication itself.

Goldschmied described to listeners to the Radio 4 series *Tuning into Children* (1998) how babies use four methods to communicate with each other and the adults close to them:

- glancing and gazing intently
- pre-verbal noises
- exchanging objects
- mutual touching

In this chapter we explore how babies and young children communicate and listen and how this is supported through their play. This starts the debate about how practitioners in out-of-home care settings need to develop the skills to observe, listen, talk and communicate and respond more effectively, to become in tune with the baby's and young child's individual characteristics and languages (Goldschmied and Selleck 1996).

## Close up and personal

The recurring theme in this book has been about the importance of the close relationship between baby, parents and practitioners for play to begin. Long before oral language begins, babies are using all their senses to play with us, to communicate with us and to us.

Talking, though, is vital. Kotulak (1997: 33) cites the work of Huttenlocher, a psychologist at the University of Chicago, which concluded that children who are spoken to frequently by their mothers have improved language skills – babies at 20 months old who had talkative mothers knew 131 more words than infants of less talkative mothers. Four months later the chatty mothers and babies were talking away with 295 more known words than the quieter mothers and their babies.

Jackson (2002) compares Western societies, where speech is seen as a forerunner for academic success, to those cultures in which babies and young children are not talked to or included in the conversations of daily life because the close personal intimacies of handling and stroking are considered more essential for communicating. Newborn babies, as we saw earlier with the photograph of Andy and Niamh (with her mouth opening and tongue protruding), and from the work of Murray and Andrews (2000), are already imitating other facial expressions such as happiness and sadness as well as communicating through imitation.

Babies' gestures need to be carefully observed and interpreted, as some of them are so minute they will be missed. Very young babies' attention span is very short; during the first month they can only look fleetingly at objects and people's faces even when feeding. However, these babies can recognize and discriminate between their parents' voices hours after birth (Murray and Andrews 2000). We know that babies recognize sounds such as music and voices played to them whilst still in utero, and Winston demonstrated this clearly on the BBC series *Child of Our Time*, pregnant mothers were played a range of music and these pieces were played back after birth the babies responded to the music they had heard, remembering and discriminating. Later on, when those babies were about 10 months old, the music was played again and the babies responded to the music that they had heard in utero and immediately after birth. Listening, then, and the ability to listen is present before birth. Sally Ward (2000) suggests that this area is vital to the development of language and cognition but is often neglected.

## Play signs

We have already begun to explore, in Chapter 4, how babies' signals are made up of very fine movements as part of their innate need to communicate, and how systems of baby signs have been developed to support this. Signing systems have been developed for babies with hearing and non-hearing. Parents and practitioners all recognize the gesture from a baby who wants to be fed and sounds linked to the physical functions of feeding and being comfortable. Babies begin to learn the responses and to respond to these gestures, the immediate attention from nearby adults, action resulting in handling for feeding or changing or playing. This is where the beginnings of conversations or 'protoconversations' (Trevarthen 1998: 90) take place, using facial gestures and movements, turn-taking, smiling and imitating. It is in this play between baby and adult of talking, listening, responding, replying, that the basis for speech patterns begins. Babies are listening and playing with sounds, beginning to understand how conversations are organized. Playing games such as 'peep-bo' and give and take encourage conversation and turn-taking. Bruner's work (1976) demonstrated that mothers were the key players in these early kinds of games with babies, and that they were supporting the baby to learn language by being the instigator in the games. However, Trevarthen (1998: 88) suggests that babies can learn to join in games and 'dance like body play' with willing adults mirroring the babies' play. His work has highlighted the joint action in close relationships where the baby is and can be the leader in the play. It would appear that the baby is in charge of these play conversations and dances, sometimes initiating and sometimes following the lead, perhaps without us being aware of it.

The *English Birth to Three Matters Framework* (2002) suggests that practitioners supporting babies and young children to become sociable and effective communicators should note how adults and other children respond, through mirroring, echoing and interpreting and sharing objects, offering objects as a way of making friendships with adults and children. Some practitioners may need to begin to play more closely with the babies and young children they work with, to enable them to read these tiny signals and respond to them.

## Babies initiating play; adults listening and tuning in ■

Reflect again on Rebecca, aged 10 months, in Chapter 4. Her request for the play to be repeated so that she could join in was recognized and responded to. This is about tuning in to the baby's gestures and individual play needs.

Young (2003: 39) carried out two research projects on music in the early years; here she observes an alert and responsive practitioner responding to the play needs of a baby aged 11 months. The baby is bouncing up and down on an inflatable floor cushion. She calls rhythmically 'er, er, er' and 'Mmmmm ...' as she bounces. A practitioner across the room responds 'Bouncy, bouncy, Flora, are you bouncing up and down?' The baby's key person is engaged feeding another baby, but she moves in closer to Flora, still feeding, and chants 'Bouncy, bouncy, up and down, Bouncy, bouncy, off to town' (a familiar knee bouncing rhyme in this setting). She then looks at the baby in her lap and says 'Bouncy, bouncy'. Young observes that this is said much more slowly and in a different tone.

Here the practitioner is interacting and responding with both of her key children who have different immediate needs; this is often a delicate balancing act for any practitioner or parent. However, the key person was encouraged by her colleague to respond to Flora's needs, and having moved in delicately she was able to support Flora's play and to feed the baby. The practitioner also changes tone, skilfully and appropriately, for a baby in the middle of a feed does not want to begin to play a knee-bouncing game. Flora enjoyed an immediate response to her own rhythmical play, with the practitioners offering the oral language describing her movement, extending the play experience and acknowledging her enjoyment.

## Responsive play partners ■

Practitioners in settings working with groups of babies sometimes need to support each other in the interpretations of and responses to babies' needs. More experienced practitioners can support those new to the play of babies and young children. Rebecca's and Flora's practitioners were observant, responsive and aware; aware of babies sometimes subtle (with Rebecca) and noisier (Flora) interchanges reminding adults that they are there and ready to play. This intimate, responsive behaviour is crucial and critical for the beginnings of play and the right of every baby and young child in group care to be acknowledged as an individual.

## Tuning in

The *Tuning into Children* (1999) tapes have wonderful conversations between babies and parents, which when we take time to listen to, can help with our understanding of the need for these conversations and their place in early play. Very young babies are clearly listening and responding to parents' conversations. And babies don't mind what we talk to them about, the weather, the garden, what is going to happen next, who is coming to see them today; the 'verbal diarrhoea' as one practitioner called it, or running commentary of daily life, is vital to babies developing listening and language skills.

Most experts seem agreed that to encourage and promote language being close to the baby and child is vital. Crystal (1986: p59) and Trevarthen (2001) identify eye contact as essential, Crystal says that 'talking to' should mean 'looking at', and babies need us to look at them whilst we talk, and real communication will begin. This can be a challenge when there are other babies and young children wanting or trying to talk to you. Babies and young children need the close contact of familiar adult voices, they want to listen to and begin to make sense of the conversations. Crystal advises that it takes time to get used to a new face and a new voice, so in group settings babies and young children need the constancy of a familiar adult to support their language development. Trevarthen suggests that we should consider the 'emotional musicality' of the parent's voice when talking to their baby. Baby talk has its own melody and pitch, and babies respond and synchronize with the parent's sounds. His filming of very young babies with their parents demonstrates this clearly. In one, a baby of 10 weeks initiates responses and responds to his father's singing. A second video of a baby who is blind shows that he listens intently as his mother sings whilst feeding him. The baby responds to the pitch and the rhythms of her singing and begins to conduct in perfect time. Trevarthen's work with Malloch, a musician, identified the relationship between parents and babies in singing play, that with a similar sense of time, and the variations in pitch, and quality of sounds, were in fact making music together. Only unlike musicians who plan and practise together before a concert, baby and parent simply improvise, and due to the strong, intrinsic appreciation of movement, vocal expression and emotional togetherness, they perform in perfect harmony.

## Adults talking; babies playing

Motherese or Infant Directed Speech (IDS) is that affectionate baby talk that almost everyone automatically lapses into when talking to babies. Without realizing it, or practising it, parents and many practitioners automatically use this sort of speech. Trevarthen (2001) describes it as having a rich musical quality with a clear rhythm and melody. This kind of speech emphasizes vowel sounds, and research by Kuhl found that it follows the same rules in English, Russian and Swedish. Kuhl discovered that in all three languages the mothers talked to their babies using exaggerated vowel sounds, which enable babies' brains to quickly absorb the information. Babies then begin to use the same sounds and the research concluded that 'language input to infants has culturally universal characteristics designed to promote language learning'. This kind of speech attracts and maintains babies' attention (Hawkes 1999).

Listen to parents and experienced practitioners talking to babies and young children and we will observe:

- their speech is slower than normal;
- there are more pauses, allowing for response from the baby;
- it is more tuneful, changing pitch, soft and loud, almost sing-songy;
- they listen to the babies' vocalizations, the silence encouraging the baby to take their turn;
- they repeat babies' sounds back to them – maintaining attention and communicating to the baby how important they are in this play and conversation;
- they watch what the baby is looking at, following their gaze or eye pointing, giving them the language – 'that's the wind blowing the blinds, phew, phew, phew', or 'oh, that's Big Ted on the chair, hello Big Ted, say hello to Harry'.
(Trevarthen 2001, Gopnik et al 1999)

Listening to and watching parents play with their babies and young children will help practitioners to use and maintain the gestures and language from home. Goldschmied and Selleck (1996) suggest that some kinds of affectionate play seen in some cultures may not always be appropriate, play such as squeezing and pinching babies faces. Singing and playing games, which reflect different cultural traditions need to be debated in the setting and collections made of a range and variety. Those first games, where practitioners play blowing raspberries on tummies or anticipatory play where baby is not quite sure whether it is the tummy or the leg that will be tickled or kissed, may not always be appropriate for some families.

These are for many the stuff of babies play. However, when playing with other peoples babies, parents need to know that these are the sort of games played daily in the setting, that they are comfortable with them. Practitioners need to be aware of different styles of parenting, thinking about different smells, tastes, music and talk, maintaining dual language experiences through everyday familiar words in the early years setting. These are the babies' 'hundred languages' and practitioners and parents can play and work together, learning new words, signs and translating simple repetitive games.

## Crying

Although for the practitioner hearing the baby they are caring for crying and becoming upset can be distressing, crying is an important tool for the baby. Jackson (2002: 275) cites a Russian proverb that tells if a baby does not cry, the mother does not know what it wants. Crying is an important part of the baby's 'call and response' system. Parents quickly become tuned in to their baby's different cries and are usually able to respond appropriately. Babies have three distinct cries identified; Smith and Cowie (1991: 283) describe them as:

- a basic crying pattern, quiet to begin with, intermittent but becomes louder and more rhythmical, it is usually associated with hunger;
- an angry cry, much as above, but has longer sounds and longer pauses between the sounds;
- a pain cry, a long cry followed by a long silence and gasps. It is sudden and loud from the start.

Families will respond differently to baby's cries depending on the family culture. Practitioners need to be aware of the different responses families have to their baby's cries (Goldschmied and Jackson 1994, Goldschmied and Selleck 1996).

There needs to be debate around the issues of babies crying and how it makes the practitioner feel. It can be quite difficult and challenging for some practitioners, reminding them perhaps of painful personal incidents in their own childhood, or the need for non-judgement of other families' parenting styles.

Jackson (2002) observes how Western parents have a bad press with regards to babies' crying. In South America, India and Africa amazement is expressed at the Western babies' capacity for crying and parents' inability to soothe their babies and the strategies for leaving babies to cry. Babies in some cultures hardly cry at all: Gusii babies in Kenya cry less than half as much as American babies.

Babies will and do cry, and those other significant adults need to know how to respond and what sort of response is appropriate for that baby and their family culture. Alice's key person, Sarah, was observed doing just that on several occasions around the treasure basket play. A crying baby cannot play and needs support.

## Tuning out, listening in

We need to ensure that babies and young children play where there is low-level background noise. This might seem impossible in group-care settings, however the environment should be planned to offer opportunities for babies to have quieter space as well as the noisier activities. Background noise such as the radio needs caution. Babies cannot tune out background sounds and even at 3 months old cannot focus on foreground sounds. They are beginning to enjoy listening to music, which can be a rich source of carefully used sounds for play experiences.

As babies begin to recognize familiar sounds and finding the source of sounds they will turn to tune in to people and sounds. Babies will turn to familiar voices more frequently, and at around five months they begin to respond to familiar sounds, getting excited about the sound of the car or door keys. This is another opportunity for playing 'who's this or what's that sound then' games, tuning them into the car pulling up on the drive, the phone ringing or the key in the door. In the setting practitioners need to describe what is happening around the babies, 'here comes Mary to see us, she has brought the clean laundry' and 'Time to put the kettle on and make someone a feed I think' or 'Look, who is at the window, can you see Sally, shall we go over and say hello?'

By about six months babies begin to listen and look at the same time (Carter 1999). To support this, practitioners need to be aware that when the baby is playing they cannot listen and play. So asking the baby questions such as 'what are you doing, or is that nice?' is irrelevant. You will see that the baby does not even look up. They can't, unless they stop playing. And we don't want to stop play.

The need for getting close up and personal has already been addressed, however it is important. Babies are able to distinguish between male and female voices by about two months (Greenfield 2000), so if you are using recorded songs in out-of-home settings try to offer those with male and female voices. For some babies in out-of-home care settings we need to be aware that they may be limited in the diversity of voices they hear, if the majority of the practitioners are female. This could explain why sometimes we notice babies in out-of-home care settings being startled or very interested when a different sounding voice is heard. Babies love to hear parents and practitioners singing, and they do not mind whether we are tuneful or not. Singing reassures them that you are there and encourages them to listen. Real voices should be heard more frequently than the recorded ones. Babies need adults to be expressive, to use wide gestures to communicate, illustrate and demonstrate when talking with babies. Many practitioners use IDS and very expressive gestures without being aware of it.

## Play routines: enhancing daily routines

Playing during changing times, games such as find the nappy and here comes the cotton wool, as baby is changed and made fun are important for babies. For babies in group settings this personal time is also a very important one-to-one time, so practitioners need to plan in time for conversations and with babies and young children, opportunities to tell them what is happening or about to happen, giving them the opportunity to be independent and contribute to their care needs. Bearing in mind the work of Trevarthen on the musicality of young children as they play, practitioners need to talk, sing and play – making up games and songs for an event. We had one just for nappy changing in our house and Laura can still hum it today with a gentle reminder! Having songs that are part of daily routine also help babies and young children to understand the passing of the day or to signal certain events – but don't sing simply for that reason, sing to share the pleasure that babies and young children get from your voice and to begin to play at making their own sounds.

## Is that nice dear?

Babies and young children will enjoy the play language that accompanies new experiences. The sand, water, gloop can all be opportunities for practitioners to support play with appropriate language. However, what involved and absorbed babies and toddlers do not need – and will probably not listen to – is the low-level questioning that can accompany some play activities. The treasure basket is not the place to begin talking to babies about the feel or smell of an object – they cannot listen and play, so it is important to allow them the full play aspect of the basket. However, introducing some of the objects from the basket to play in a different way or to use with a small group of babies and young children is quite different and should not be confused with treasure basket play. I prefer to use the term 'exploratory or interest baskets' when using collections of objects with older children who have developed enough language to question and talk about the objects. I have used baskets that contain objects of similar materials or sets, or colours.

## Playing with others

Babies and young children need no encouragement to play together, young children love to be near older children and there are many opportunities in group settings for babies, young children and older children to play together. Meeting up at mealtimes is one aspect of the day particularly when siblings can be together, however there are many babies and young children who are only children. These children especially need the opportunity to play with children older and younger than themselves. Here children's oral language will take off as they enjoy social play and interactions. Babies will enjoy watching other children play. Let the babies sit safely strapped in prams or buggies – for short periods, and watch what is going around them. The outside environment is important as well. Babies love to be outside, where new smells, sights, offer the beginnings of a whole new multisensory play experience. Toddlers too will enjoy the opportunity to watch older children play; however, after time spent watching, they may well want to join in and might need the support of a friendly older child or a sensitive adult to introduce them to the play.

Offer mobile babies and young children a well-stocked role-play area with real-sized play materials and familiar items from their homes and community. A large box of hats, handbags, shopping bags, waistcoats, chunky necklaces, and a full length mirror will all contribute to playing about who am I and who are you ... and look at me now.

## That's nice dear

As language development begins to explode, so to does the speed with which excited young children try to share their new experiences, and they need time for us to listen and give them the language for those experiences. It has happened to every early years practitioner, a child desperate to tell you about or show you something they have found in the garden – usually dead, nearly dead, dirty, alive and creeping or crawling along, or a new flower, seed head,

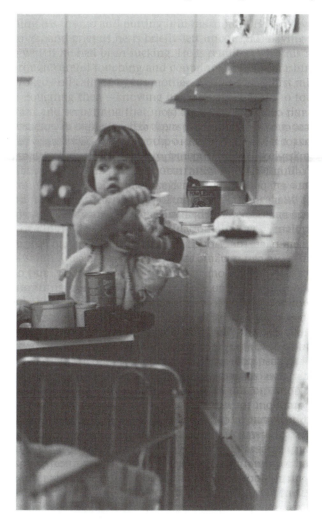

*Tea time.*

puddle, all the things children under three find fascinating. They tell you as soon as they can get to you, either with it in tow, or dragging you off to admire it. They show and tell every adult who visits during the day, either outside or inside. And of course the other children become involved and they want to share this new find. So lots of children are showing the 'new find' to lots of people. Practitioners need to remember, no matter how many times you have been behind the shed to admire the hundreds of baby snails or the 'normus snaky thingy' (a slow worm I was shown), for the child who is telling you at that precise moment it may be the first time that they have shared the news. They may well tell you something new or different, or they may not have the language and want you to look at it with them and tell them what all the excitement is about. It may be that child's first attempt at conversation or communication. They need encouragement and support, not to lose the moment with 'That's nice dear' or 'I have already seen the snails today'. They need to feel valued and have a sense of self contributing to conversations and events, and being 'good enough' (Griffin 1987).

## No literacy hour here please

### *Song play*

Songs, stories and rhymes are critical to babies' and young children's language play. Make sure you sing familiar songs and rhymes regularly, offering repetition and action play to support the song. Actions can be created for many rhymes and songs, early years practitioners need to be creative and inventive to encourage young children to stay involved in singing sessions. Using songs throughout the day as you do other things is a good way of keeping songs and rhymes as part of the day, not a hurried 'on the carpet slot' whilst the tables are being laid, when young children are hungry or tired – or both, or waiting for the 'bathroom run'. Singing sessions should be timed to meet the needs of the babies and young children. Young (2003) also suggests that music with babies in their first year should be tied into everyday play.

Babies can enjoy playing movement games and songs with another baby and adult or in a small group of three. Older babies can play for longer, however practitioners need to plan. Make sure you know what you are going to sing, that all the adults know all the words – it sounds obvious but if the practitioners don't know the words and actions properly, the children never will. Older babies and children love surprises and I use a very large tin (10.5 inches tall, 9.5 inches wide) that holds several puppets, a chatty bear, a sleepy teddy bear, a magic stone and other bits and pieces. The children never knew who was in the tin that day and it was kept closed until needed. Singing games can also be wonderful movement exercises for babies, with practitioners and babies on their tummies on the floor, or doing action songs with baby on your lap and giving the baby the words for the actions.

### Up and down game

Practitioner sits on floor legs straddled wide apart, holding the baby firmly under arms. Some practitioners may find it more comfortable to sit against a wall or have a bean bag as back support.

Up up up into the sky we go *(lift baby up in the air in your arms facing outwards)*
Down, down, down on to our tummies we go *(gently bring him down on his tummy)*
Roly-poly, tickle that back
Turn Harry (name baby) over and clap clap clap *(clap baby's hand together and then yours)*

Words and actions: Ruth Forbes (2002)

### Name that tune

Babies and toddlers love singing; they often find it easier to sing than to talk, settings need a repertoire of familiar songs to sing regularly. If you introduce lots of new songs in a session, the toddlers will be lost. Introduce one or two new songs in a week and ensure you practice them daily. Young (2003: 44) describes the characteristics of play songs for babies as identified by Trehub and Schellenberg (1995). These include

- having a faster tempo;
- having a more animated style;
- the words are key to the song;
- the rhythms are more closely linked with the words;
- gestures are included to illustrate the words;
- they involve active participation with the baby once he is ready.

Young describes babies' musical play features, which help the baby to engage with an adult; these include anticipation, surprise, teasing, laughing and having fun. Anticipations and repetitions are important and most practitioners can identify favourite play songs that include these, such as 'Incy-wincy spider'. Finding new games to play to support the babies' and young child's developing communication and listening skills is important. Practitioners can also be creative by using well-known tunes and rhythms with words that suit the event or the setting. One playgroup setting I knew used the tune of 'Here comes the bride' to announce

'Here comes our snack
What's on the plate?
Here comes our snack
Don't you be late'
          (Author unknown 1987)


## Once upon a time

> ... the child was not understanding the language ... I saw this 4
> month old struggling to turn the page because it's such fun,
> because there is something greater on the other side. The baby
> had learned ... by the interaction with the mother ... this is a
> fun thing to do ... This child is going to love books.
>               (*Tuning into Children* 1999: 91, Elizabeth Bates
>                           University of California)

The importance of books and stories cannot be under estimated in
babies and young children's language play. The baby in the quote
above was on a plane, looking at a bright, colourful, book for babies.
Bates believes that reading to young children is one of the best things
we can do. The content of the book is not critical; it is the interplay
between adult and child that is so important. As well as acquiring
new language, the beginnings of recognizing books for pleasure and
enjoyment can be shared with even the youngest baby. The two
children with childminder in the *English Birth to Three Matters
Framework* video (2002) are having a wonderful book play experience. The baby joins in, 'finding his voice', the older child's bi-lingual
learning is responded to and the whole episode is intimate and
pleasurable. The rhythms and the patterns of the adults voice as she
tells the story, the interplay as the child points to pages in the book
and the baby agreeing, when the story comes to an end that it's all
over.

Telling stories to babies and very young children using expressive
gestures and voices brings the story to life. Babies will keenly
anticipate the turning of the pages when they are part of a one-to-
one book play experience. Being close to the familiar adult is also
important, a chance to snuggle in and feel very special. Babies and
toddlers will enjoy tales of other small babies and children and
practitioners can create stories around the children in the setting,
these will be enjoyed. Storytelling can add to the children's play
experiences as they move in to the two to three year age group, listen
and observe as they begin to play in the role-play or home corner
areas using small narratives to describe the action.

Book baskets or boxes can be available for the youngest of babies to help themselves to. In one experiment where books had always been displayed but out of babies reach in a setting, the practitioners used low cardboard boxes on the floor to contain books. The mobile, crawling and toddling babies soon went to explore. Babies were observed sitting turning the babies, 'reading' the pages and one baby of 8 months was captured on the video holding the book with one hand and then lifting the book towards her, she turned her wrist 180 degrees and then began 'telling' the story to the room. When the video tape was watched again more closely and some recording of one of the practitioners was observed, we saw that the baby was imitating the exact hand movement used by her key person when showing a book to two or three babies. The hand movement was unmistakable as identical to Liz's, a gracious, long wristed hand movement.

The setting went on to improve the boxes, covering them with sturdy sticky backed plastic and using the pages (laminated) from damaged books to label the box. The babies' interest in books was maintained and the babies were encouraged and supported to:

- make real choices and decisions about which space they wanted to play in the baby room;
- choose their own books;
- look at the books with or without an adult.

The practitioners still read and told stories to the babies during the day, either on a one to one basis or in small groups.

## Key points from this chapter

- Listen well and observe closely;
- Recognize that babies and young children will communicate in many different ways;
- Begin to tune into signals, sounds and language of the babies and young children you play with;
- Adults need to keep a running commentary of what they are doing when with babies and young children;
- Background noise needs to be minimized, constant music in the background is not appropriate for settings with babies and toddlers;
- Have song play at special times;
- But sing with the babies and young children as you play through the day;
- Listening skills need to be encouraged and promoted in our youngest children.

# 10

# CONTINUING THE DEBATE ABOUT BABIES BEGINNING TO PLAY

This chapter will focus on the threads woven through this book and debated about babies' play.

The LEGO℗ Educational Division use four headings to describe their approach to support young children's play and learning process. These headings are:

Connect – Construct – Contemplate – Continue

I have included a further heading of 'communication', which, put between contemplate and continue, can help us to focus our thinking about babies beginning to play and pull together important aspects from this book. Communication, both the child's and the adult's, is an important part of this focus.

I am not part of the debate that asks 'do babies play?', I believe they do, and from the time before they are born. Researchers and early years experts appear to collaborate this (Goldschmied and Jackson 1994; Trevarthen 1998, 2000; Forbes 1999b, 1999c; Gopnik et al. 1999; Murray and Andrews 2000; Bruce 2003). Babies play with their own bodies when they are still in utero, at birth they immediately look for people and objects closest to them, both proximally and in relationships. They watch, absorb, internalize and then begin to play with information or ideas, testing out themselves, other people and objects.

## Making Connections

Babies need to develop strong neural connections in order for brain growth and development to occur. We know it is the little synaptic jump or pulse from one cell to another that is so vital for building up this dense layer of neural connections – storing up all the babies experiences and exposures to the world. We also know that rich and abundant play, experienced in daily life, is the best kind of experience for young babies and children (Carter 1999; Gopnik et al. 1999; Blakemore 2000; Selleck 2001; Thorp 2003). They begin to connect ideas and understanding through their rich play experiences with people and the environment. Like energetic scientists, these young babies and children search for patterns, sorting, classifying, comparing and categorizing. They begin making links, predictions, exploring and experimenting to try and make sense of the world.

We have debated the need for strong connections between babies and adults, particularly those outside the immediate family, those other significant adults or key people in an out-of-home setting who will be the connectors, encouraging babies' play to begin in a new environment. The play will be with some familiar and some new materials and resources.

These strong and healthy connections with constant, consistent adults are the anchors for future brain development and growth. They are essential for young children growing and developing a strong sense of emotional wellbeing, feeling valued and safe. Relationships need to be made and developed. Practitioners who consider the importance of these relationships for rich play experiences to develop in the setting, make sure that they have connected with families to build on the play and routines from home. Making Connections is a component part of a Competent Learner in the *English Birth to Three Matters Framework* (2002). The focus here is on connections between senses and movement, finding out about other people and becoming involved and engaged in play.

Practitioners will also need to consider their own personal feelings and thoughts about looking after other peoples' young babies, being non-judgemental about the work-life balance of families, parenting styles and skills, and instead to support and make suggestions for the continuing play and learning of the family (Forbes 1999a; Elfer 2001).

Responsive and reflective practitioners work to try to make strong connections with the families of the babies and young children they share in the care of; listening, talking, observing, and sharing experiences. They will need to be emotionally literate, secure in their own knowledge of the individual needs of these very young children.

Connecting regularly with colleagues and practitioners from other settings for wider discussion and debates on the provision, policies and observations of young babies' and children will influence and have an effect on their developing play.

Work such as the *English Birth to Three Matters Framework* (2002) and *Key Times* (Manning-Morton 2001) has begun to raise the profile of children up to 3 and we need to make sure that these very young children and babies can begin to play and are enabled and encouraged to be in charge of their own play and learning.

## Constructing information from the real world

Babies and young children enjoy opportunities and experiences to think and become thinkers; they need time to construct from real-life experiences, which will in turn build or construct their brain. Earlier in the book the plasticity (flexibility) of the young developing brain was identified, and rich play experiences can help to construct and re-construct the brain.

If we are to give these very youngest babies and children opportunities for constructing knowledge of themselves and the world, it needs to be in a framework of self-confidence, where the environment is one of 'have a go', where children have the freedom to explore and play, finding out the how and why. Knoop (2002) tells us that mistakes are for learning and creating from. If we think about Bruce's (1991: 58) definition of free flow play, where children are able to use, integrate and apply their knowledge and understanding, then free flow play is where we would expect to see children creating and learning from first-hand experiences, which will include 'mistakes'. Bruce (1991: 79) also reminds us that free flow play is a place where children 'gain control over their lives, and over knowledge and understanding, and feelings and relationships with each other'. Goleman (1996: 90) describes flow as 'the neurobiology of excellence'. It is where emotional intelligence is at its best, he says 'in flow the emotions are not just contained and chaneled, but positive, energized and aligned with the task at hand'. It reminds us of how it might feel to be so involved and immersed in whatever we are doing, for an adult it might be a sport or a hobby, for a child playing, or involved in an activity, time stands still and nothing else is relevant.

It would appear that to be involved in a task or an activity that is within our capabilities but still offers an amount of challenge, still demanding that extra nugget of thought, or skill, is essential.

Babies and very young children need time to play, so that free flow play will emerge and develop. Observations of some very young babies under 1 year old at play identified and confirmed several aspects of free flow as described by Bruce (1991, 2002) already emerging in their play. The babies used first-hand experiences, chose to play, played alone and with other babies, had personal play agendas, were deeply involved and tried out recent learning. Practitioners able to recognize some of these aspects debated and planned for further opportunities and offered resources, spaces and time for the babies to begin to play. (Forbes 1999c).

Knoop (2002: 50) offers a definition of flow as 'a condition in which we are completely engrossed in a game or task, lose our sense of time and place, and utilize our learning potential to the fullest'. He offers flow as 'the natural balance between challenges and skills'. Flow can only happen in high-challenge, low-risk play environments, where practitioners plan for, provide and respond to the changing and developing play needs of young children. Babies or young children struggling with inappropriate play experiences or resources such as 'art activities' are not experiencing anything like being in flow, they will be anxious, fretful, wanting to please the adult they care so much for. Think instead of the toddlers trail-making – no anxiety here, pure pleasure and delight in themselves and the environment, the whole play experience flowing, and personal well-being high.

The *English Birth to Three Matters Framework* (2002) offers practitioners constructive and positive ways to begin to provide play and practical support to these very young children through video examples of practice.

Practitioners should consider how they find out about and include young children's opinions, thoughts and feelings as they plan for the play and learning in the setting. They will need to make sure that families are included in the debates and that ideas from home, where possible, are carried out in the setting. Babies and young children can be constructors of materials, ideas, thoughts and information. They need to be able to de-construct as well – work things abstractly or physically – knock down the bricks and start again without feeling put down or that the 'building', or more importantly themselves, were not good enough. There should be no fear of failure; it's just about doing something again a different way. When we use open questions with young children, the answers may not always be the ones we had in mind, they might not be the 'wrong' answer, just a different one. Similarly, we should not have our own pre-determined 'constructions' or offer didactic play resources or experiences, always adult-led and product-motivated. Sensitive, reflective practitioners will make sure that they are offering appropriate play experiences.

Encouraging independent thinking is part of the construction process, where even very young children can be part of decision-making, in groups or individually, for example in discussions that address real problems – what shall we do?, how shall we share the crackers or fruit at snack time? are there too many children in the role-play area?. Very young children can and should be involved in the sorts of decisions that affect their day and their play. Using persona dolls, as introduced by Babette Brown, or a special teddy at circle time, can be helpful in enabling young children to work out solutions to real problems or their own emotional struggles.

The construction of the environment offered to babies and young children is important. In order to encourage these young children to experience free flow play, opportunities to become involved and absorbed in play, the materials and resources need to be carefully constructed but not manipulated. Consider the layout of the play spaces, trying new and different things, offering a rich, multi-sensory play environment.

Play opportunities and experiences need to be imaginative; there needs to be music and singing as discussed earlier in the book, laughter from (not at) both adults and children, a sense of being comfortable for all the children and adults, a place where babies' and very young children's individual and specific needs are respected and responded to. However, these individual 'needs' must be identified and responded to by innovative practitioners, in a setting where there is a sense of fun and pleasure, with adults who want to work with and be with these very young children. Then the play really will begin.

## Contemplating and communicating about babies' play

Time is needed for contemplation or reflection on babies' play experiences. A few minutes talking time at the end or beginning of the day or during a quiet naptime, can be wisely used. It can prove invaluable, particularly when thoughts and actions are documented for further reflection. Planned regular team meetings without the distractions of the working day are essential for opportunities of deeper reflection and discussion. This thinking and talking time with other practitioners and colleagues can support practitioner learning, and will of course affect the play experience and provision for the babies and young children.

Just as we can encourage and enable very young children to con-tribute to the discussions about their play and learning, we should try to begin to encourage these young children to reflect on their play and deepen their understanding of their play experiences. Close observation, talking with and listening to these very young children, will enable practitioners to contemplate further, thinking, debating and evaluating the play experiences – what else could we offer to extend the play interest?, is there somewhere we could visit with the children?, why might this child be playing in this way?, do we need to seek out further advice or information. Listening to children's ideas and opinions as Penny Lancaster (2004) has been doing with children over 3, demonstrates a respect and valuing of children's own experiences. It means their voices will be heard and their experiences will shape and perhaps change policy and practice.

Practitioners will reflect on their own and the setting's practice, to discuss, debate and collaborate with parents as well as colleagues on the babies' play, communicating ideas, feelings and thoughts with other adults who have deeper knowledge and different theories and experience. Sharing experiences, clarifying thoughts and ideas, and talking about the play experiences of the day are essential.

Contemplation has to include communication and a commitment from practitioners to find out more – perhaps about a developing schema pattern, and to plan then for their own further learning and the babies' and young children's play experiences.

## Continue the debate and let the play begin

> A society can be judged by its attitude to its youngest children.
> (Goldschmied and Jackson 1994: 1)

Continuing the debate on babies beginning to play has to include the bigger picture of social policy and attitudes to our youngest children. Babies and families are not always able to play together, families need financial support in order to make choices about whether to return to employment following the birth of a baby. For many families the option of staying at home with their very young children is not available, with many women particularly identifying that if given the option they would not return to work whilst their children are under 3.

The Starting Strong Report (Bennett 2003) identified that 34 per cent of children in the UK under 3 years of age are cared for in formal childcare settings, with an expansion in publicly funded provision since 1997. However these figures do not take in to account informal childcare and the significant increase in provision in the UK since 1997.

The changes in parental leave have also given families more choices about sharing the care at home (Bennett 2003).

The Starting Strong report identified the persistent division between care and education still facing many of the 20 governments who took part in the review, with barriers to parental needs and the development of young children. One of the barriers identified is the opposition by those working in the education sector to take on the care needs of children under 3. This has a strong historical background and one which is not going to be resolved easily.

Our European counterparts have lower levels of adults with low literacy and numeracy than the UK (Moser 1999). We know from research such as Starting Strong (Bennett 2003) and from practice in early years settings that adults make a big difference to the play and learning of young children. Adults are crucial. However, the complex lives that many children and families live today appears to be having an effect on particularly their speech and language skills, speaking and listening. A report on BBC television news identified that 89 per cent of parents had concerns or worries over their children's speech and language. A campaign by the national educational charity for children with speech and language difficulties, I CAN, called Chatterbox Challenge, focuses on language development of young children through stories, games, finger-plays and rhyme, sharing ways with families to support language skills through play. Many families need this support, with more nuclear families and less contact with the extended family; songs, stories and games are no longer part of every-day life. For many families the skills of living in poor housing, financial and environmental concerns are more relevant than the play and learning of their young children. Some young parents may not have experienced a rich language environment themselves, and so have little experience of nursery rhymes, songs and games that are essential in early language play, to share with their children. Wells (2003) suggests that many of the adults with low levels of literacy and numeracy come from families where parents took very little interest in the education of their children and that these adults had 'often failed at school before they'd even had a chance to succeed'.

The Basic Skills Agency has many programmes working with Neighbourhood Nurseries and Sure Start to support early years practitioners with the work they do with families, to identify and support families with low levels of literacy and numeracy through encouraging families to become involved in their children's learning and play. These programmes aim to break the cycle of poor literacy and numeracy and decrease the current high numbers of adult low-level literacy and numeracy.

In Sweden, Denmark and Finland, children start school at age 6 years. The provision here for children under three is mostly subsidised and the emphasis is very much on the development of social skills – such as the importance and need for close relationships with children and adults, understanding and responding to children's signals, self-confidence, self-esteem, self-respect, awareness of children learning through their senses and children's rights to appropriate provision and adults to nurture and care (Jensen 1994; Griffin 1997).

Many of these aspects are beginning to be more highly valued in the UK, and underpin some of the frameworks for current thinking. Practitioners will need to debate and identify the theoretical perspectives and aspects that fit their setting, community and culture.

We need to consider how as a society and in our culture we respond to our youngest citizens. Babies and young children are entitled to respect and respectful provision; where they are encouraged and enabled to explore and play independently supported by close, trusting adults. No 'hurrying up' – runner beans planted earlier don't grow any taller or stronger than those planted at the right time, the ground isn't warm enough to nurture the roots.

Elinor Goldschmied, in the foreword to this book, said 'it is crucial that we hold on to the key needs of very young babies and children ensuring that their emotional development is supported in a warm, unhurried manner'. The debate around the support for parents' and practitioners' continued learning about play needs to move on. Then, and only then, we will observe and enjoy babies really beginning to play.

# BIBLIOGRAPHY AND VIDEOS

Abbot, L. and Moylett, H. (1997) *Working with the Under-3s: Responding to Children's Needs*. Buckingham: Open University Press.

Abbott, L. and Rodger, R. (eds) (1997) *Quality Education in the Early Years*. Buckingham: Open University Press.

Arthur, C. (1999) Additives in toys linked to cancer, *The Independent*, 14 January.

Athey, C. (1990) *Extending Thought in Young Children*. London: Paul Chapman Publishing.

Atkinson, P. (2003) Baby walkers are they a danger to young children?, *Early Childhood Practice*, Vol. 5, No.1: 7–11.

Babies in Art (1997) London and Basingstoke: Macmillan.

Ball, C. (1992) *Start Right*. London: Royal Society of Arts.

Barnes, D. (1998) Play in historical contexts, in D. Fromberg and D. Bergen (eds) *Play from Birth to Twelve and Beyond. Contexts, Perspectives, and Meanings*. New York and London: Garland Publishing.

Bates, E. (1999) Becoming Literate in *Tuning into Children: Understanding a Child's Development From Birth to 5 years*. (Pocket book and audio tapes to accompany series) National Children's Bureau/ BBC Education/BBC Radio 4

BBC (1999) Panorama: Romania.

BBC (2004) Breakfast News 30/1/04

BBC Child of Our Time 2002/3

Bennett, J. (2003) Starting Strong the persistent division between care and education. *Early Childhood Research* Vol 1 No 1 May 03 Sage Publications

Birth to Three Matters: (2002) A Framework to Support Children in their Earliest Years. Sure Start

Blakemore, C. (1998) Brain development and research findings. Unpublished conference paper, Early Years Conference Pen Green Centre, 28 January.

Blakemore, C. (2000) Early learning and the brain. Unpublished paper, RSA Lecture, 14 February.

Bodrova, E. and Long, D. L. (1998) Play with objects, in D. Fromberg and D. Bergen (eds) *Play from Birth to Twelve and Beyond. Contexts, Perspectives, and Meanings*. New York and London: Garland Publishing.

Bowlby, J. (1969) *Attachment and Loss*. Vol.1, *Attachment*. London: Hogarth Press.

Bredekamp, S. and Copple, C. (eds) (1997) *Developmentally Appropriate Practice in Early Childhood Programs*. Washington: National Association for the Education of Young Children.

Brooks, E. (2000) Valley of the Dolls, *The National Trust Magazine*, Number 90, Summer.

Bruce, T. (1987; 2nd edn 1997) *Early Childhood Education*. London: Hodder and Stoughton.

Bruce, T. (1991) *Time to Play in Early Childhood Education*. London: Hodder and Stoughton.

Bruce, T. (1997) Adults and children developing play together, *European Early Childhood Education Research Journal*, Vol.5, No.1: 89–99.

Bruce, T. and Meggitt, C. (2002) *Childcare and Education*, 3rd edn. London: Hodder and Stoughton.

Bruce, T. (2002) *What to look for in the play of Children Birth to Three*. Hodder and Stoughton. London

Bruer, J. (1996) Education and the brain: A bridge too far, *Educational Researcher*, Vol.26, No.8: 4–16.

Bruner, J. (1976) Learning how to do things with words, in *Human Growth and Development*. Oxford: Oxford University Press.

Candappa, Rohan (2001) *Autobiography of a One Year Old*. London: Ebury Press.

Carter, R. (1999) *Mapping the Mind*. London: Seven Dials.

Cole, M. (1998) Culture in development, in M. Woodhead, D. Faulkner and K. Littleton (eds) *Cultural Worlds of Early Childhood*. London: Routledge.

Cryer, D. and Burchinal, M. (1997) Parents as Child Care Consumers, *Early Childhood Research Quarterly*, 12: 35–58.

Crystal, D. (1986) *Listen to your Child: A Parent's Guide to Children's Language Development*. London Penguin

Curtis, A. (1994) Play in different cultures and different childhoods, in J. Moyles (ed.) *The Excellence of Play*. Buckingham: Open University Press.

David, T. et al. (2002) Review of the literature to support Birth to Three Matters: A framework to support children in their earliest years, Sure Start DfES.

Davies, M.(2003) *Helping Children to Learn Through a Movement Perspective*. (2$^{nd}$ ed) Hodder and Stoughton. London

Dixon, B. (1990) *Playing Them False: A Study of Children's Toys, Games and Puzzles*. Stoke-on-Trent: Trentham Books.

Donaldson, M. (1978) *Children's Minds*. Glasgow: Fontana/Collins.

Dowling, M. (1988) *Education 3–5*. London: Paul Chapman Publishing.

Duffy, B. (1998) *Supporting Creativity and Imagination in the Early Years*. Buckingham: Open University Press.

Dunn, J. (1993) *Young Children's Close Relationships*. London/New Delhi: Sage Publications.

Dunn, J. (1998) *The Beginning of Social Understanding*. Oxford: Blackwell.

Elfer, P. (1995) *With Equal Concern*. London: National Children's Bureau.

Elfer, P. (1996) Building Intimacy in Relationships with Young Children in Nurseries, *Early Years TACTYC*, Vol. 16, No. 2, Spring: 30–34.

Elfer, P. (2000) Babies in nurseries: exploring the 'minute particulars' of relationships made for growing, learning and inclusion. Unpublished paper presented at RNIB Conference: A Curriculum for Babies. Harrogate, 21/22 June.

Elfer, P. (2001) Attachment and the role of the key person. Unpublished paper presented at training day: Focus on Mental Health, From Birth to Primary School. Hammersmith, 15 June.

Elicker, J. (2000) A comparison of toddlers' attachment security with caregivers in childcare centers and family childcare homes. Unpublished paper presented at the XIIth Biennial International Conference in Infant Studies, Brighton, July.

Forbes, R (1993) Working with Parents. Unpublished paper, Bristol College.

Forbes, R. (1999a) Working with Families. Unpublished paper, London Metropolitan.

Forbes, R. (1999b) Action Research. Unpublished paper, London Metropolitan.

Forbes, R. (1999c) Observations. Unpublished paper, London Metropolitan.

Forbes, R. (2000) Babies in charge of their own learning: A merging and emerging curriculum. Unpublished paper, London Metropolitan.

Fromberg, D. and Bergen, D. (1998) *Play from Birth to Twelve and Beyond: Contexts, Perspectives and Meanings*. New York, London: Garland Publishing Inc.

Gardner, H. (1993) *Frames of Mind*, 2nd edn. London: Fontana/Harper.

Goddard Blythe, S. (2000) First steps to the most important ABC, *Times Educational Supplement*, 7 January.

Goddard Blythe, S. and Hyland, D. (1998) Screening for neurological dysfunction in the specific learning difficulty child, *British Journal of Occupational Therapy*, Oct. 98, 61 (10): 459–464.

Goldschmied, E. (1987) *Infants at Work. Babies of 6–9 Months Exploring Everyday Objects*, VHS Video, London: National Children's Bureau.

Goldschmied, E. (1989) Play and learning in the first year of life, in V. Williams (ed.) *Babies in Day Care: An Examination of the Issues*. London: The Daycare Trust.

Goldschmied, E. (1998) recording for *Tuning into Children*: BBC Radio 4.

Goldschmied, E. and Hughes, A. (1992) *Heuristic Play with Objects. Children of 12–20 Months Exploring Everyday Objects*. VHS Video, London: National Children's Bureau.

Goldschmied, E. and Jackson, S. (1994) *People Under Three: Young Children in Day Care*. London and New York: Routledge.

Goldschmied, E. and Selleck, D. (1996) *Communication Between Babies in their First Year*. VHS Video, London: National Children's Bureau.

Goleman, D. (1996) *Emotional Intelligence: Why It Can Matter more than IQ*. London: Bloomsbury.

Gopnik, A., Meltzoff, A. and Kuhl, P. (1999) *How Babies Think: The Science of Childhood*. London: Weidenfeld and Nicolson.

Goswami, U. (1998) *Cognition in Children*. Sussex: Psychology Press Limited.

Greenfield, S. (1999) The state of the art of the science of brain research. Unpublished paper presented at Learning and the Brain Day Conference, London, The Royal Institution, 23 November.

Greenfield, S. (2000) *Brain Story*. London: BBC Worldwide Ltd.

Greenman, J. and Stonehouse, A. (1997) *Prime Times: A Handbook for Excellence in Infant and Toddler Programs*. Melbourne: Longman.

Griffin, B. (1997) The child should feel 'good enough' – nurturing a sense of self in young children, in L. Abbot and H. Moylett (eds) *Working with the Under-3s: Responding to Children's Needs*. Buckingham: Open University Press.

Gross, R. (1997) Attachment theory extensions and applications, *Psychology Review*, Vol.4, No.2: 10–13.

Hardyment, C. (1984) *Dream Babies*. Oxford: Oxford University Press.

Hawkes, N. (1999) The Times 1/8/99

High/scope UK (1999) *The High/scope Approach For Under Threes*. VHS Video.

Holland, R. (1997) 'What's it all about?': How introducing heuristic play has affected provision for the under-threes in one day nursery, in L. Abbott and H. Moylett (eds) *Working with the Under-3s: Responding to Children's Needs*. Buckingham: Open University Press.

Hutt, S.J., Tyler, S., Hutt, C. and Christopherson, H. (1990) *Play, Exploration and Learning*. London: Routledge.

Jackson, D. (2002) *Baby Wisdom: The World's Best-kept Secrets for the First Year of Parenting*. London: Hodder and Stoughton.

Jennings, J. (2002) Implications for visually impaired children. Unpublished paper presented at Childhood Play: Foundations for Adult Creativity and Imagination. RNIB Conference, Brecon, 17 September.

Jensen, C. (1994) Fragments for a discussion about quality, in P. Moss and A. Pence (eds) *Valuing Quality in Early Childhood Services*. London: Paul Chapman Publishing.

Knoop, H.H. (2002) *Play, Learning and Creativity*. Aschehoug: Norhaven.

Kotulak, R. (1997) *Inside the Brain. Revolutionary Discoveries of How the Mind Works*. Kansas City: Andrews McMeel Publishing.

Laevers, F., Vandenbussche, E. Kog, M., Depondt, L. (1997) A process-oriented child monitoring system for young children. Experiential Education Series, No 2. Centre for Experiential Education

Lancaster, P.(2003) Listening to children project. Coram Family-DfES Sure Start London

Lancaster, P.,Broadbent, V.(2004) Listening to Young Children Resource Pack OUP. Maidenhead

LEGO℗ (2003) Explore Activity Book. Denmark: LEGO Educational Division.

Longthorn, F. (1998) *A Sensory Curriculum for Very Special People*. Human Horizons Series.

MacFarlane, A. (1975). Olfaction in the development of social preferences in the human neonate. *Ciba Foundation Symposium*

Manning-Morton, J. and Thorp, M. (2001) *Key Times – A Framework for Developing High Quality Provision for Children Under Three Years Old*. Camden Under Threes Development Group and the University of North London.

Manning-Morton, J. and Thorp, M. (2003) *A Time to Play: Playing, Growing and Learning in the First Three Years of Life*. Maidenhead, Philadelphia: Open University Press.

Matthews, J. (1994) *Helping Children to Draw and Paint in Early Childhood: Children and Visual Representation*. London: Paul Chapman Publishing

Miles, R. (1994) *The Children We Deserve. Love and Hate in the Making of the Family*. London: Harper Collins.

Millar, S. (1968) *The Psychology of Play*. London: Pelican.

Mills, C. and D. (1998) *Dispatches: The Early Years*. London: Channel 4.

Mogar, M., Nakahanta, A. and Santos Rico, S. (1999) Nurturing experiences and brain development in early childhood. Paper presented at Early Childhood Conference USA, July.

Moser, C. (1999) A Fresh Start: Improving literacy and numeracy for Adults Summary and Recommendations of the working group. DfES

Moyles, J. (ed.) (1994) *The Excellence of Play*. Buckingham, Philadelphia: Open University Press.

Murray, L. and Andrews, E. (2000) *The Social Baby*. Richmond: The Children's Project.

*National Standards for under eights in day care and childminding* (2001) DfES

Pascal, C. and Bertram, A. (1996) *The Framework for Developing Effectiveness in Early Learning Settings*. EEL Project Manual.

Penn, H. (1999) How should we care for babies and toddlers? An analysis of practice in out-of-home care for children under three. *Childcare Resource and Research Unit* Occasional Paper 10, Centre for Urban and Community Studies: University Toronto. June, iv: 66.

Piaget, J. (1962) *Play, Dreams and Imitation in Childhood*. London: Routledge and Kegan Paul.

Piaget, J. and Inhelder, B. (1969) *The Psychology of the Child*. London and Henley: Routledge and Kegan Paul.

Pinker, S. (1997) *How the Mind Works*. London: Penguin.

Post, J. and Hohmann, M. (2000) *Tender Care and Early Learning: Supporting Infants and Toddlers in Child Care Settings*. Ypsilanti: High Scope Educational Research Foundation.

Pugh, G. (ed.) (1992) *Contemporary Issues in the Early Years*. London: Paul Chapman Publishing Ltd. in association with National Children's Bureau.

Purves L. & Selleck, D. (1999) Becoming Literate in *Tuning into Children: Understanding a Child's Development From Birth to 5 years*. (Pocket book and audio tapes to accompany series) National Children's Bureau/ BBC Education/BBC Radio 4

Roberts, R. (1995) *Self-esteem and Successful Early Learning*. London: Hodder and Stoughton.

Rodd, G. (1998) *Leadership in Early Childhood*, 2nd edn. Buckingham: Open University Press.

Rutter, M. (1981) *Maternal Deprivation Reassessed*, 2nd edn. Middlesex: Penguin Books.

Selleck, D. (1997) Baby Art: Art is Me, in *Reflections on Early Education and Care. Inspired by Visits to Reggio Emilia*, Italy. BAECE

Selleck, D. (2001) 'Being Under Three Years of Age: Enhancing Quality Experience' in Pugh, G. (ed) *Contemporary Issues in the Early Years*. London: Paul Chapman Publishing Ltd. NCB

Selleck, D. and Griffin, S. (1992) Quality for Under Threes, in G. Pugh (ed.) *Contemporary Issues in the Early Years*. London: Paul Chapman Publishing Ltd.

Shore, R. (1997) *Rethinking the Brain: New Insights into Early Development*. New York: Families and Work Institute.

Smith, P. and Cowie, H. (1991) *Understanding Children's Development*, 2nd edn. Oxford: Blackwell.

Stadelhofer, K.M. and Johansen, E. (2000) *Play through the Ages: The Indoor Collections at LEGO Billund*. Denmark: Gronlund's Forlag.

Steele, H. (2001) Intergenerational patterns of attachment: recent findings from research. Unpublished paper presented at Reflexive Relationships: Encouraging Positive Parent-Child Interactions Conference, Pen Green Children's Centre, Corby, 23 March.

Stern, D. (1991) *Diary of a Baby*. London: Fontana.

Thorp, M. (2003) A Time to Play: Playing, growing and learning in the first three years of life. Paper presented at Debating Play Conference, London Metropolitan University, 12 July.

Trevarthen, C. (1998) The child's need to learn a culture, in M. Woodhead, D. Faulkner and K. Littleton (eds) *Cultural Worlds of Early Childhood*. London: Routledge.

Trevarthen, C. (2000) Communicating so babies understand for all the senses: Getting in tune with core impulses for learning. Unpublished paper presented at A Curriculum for Babies: RNIB Conference, June.

Trevarthen, C. (2001) Tuning into children: Motherese and tea-cherese, the listening voice. Unpublished paper presented at Pen Green Children's Centre, 24 March.

Vazquez, A., Manlove, E. and Vernon-Feagane, L. (2000) Childcare caregivers' thought processes and their association with quality of care: The moderating effect of different aspects of the childcare work environment. Unpublished paper presented at the XIIth Biennial International Conference in Infant Studies, Brighton, UK, July.

Vygotsky, L. (1978) *Mind in Society*. Cambridge, MA: Harvard University Press.

Ward, S. (2000) *Babytalk*. London: Century.

Wells, A. (2003) Speaking Out. *Nursery World 23/1/03 p16*

Whalley, M. (1999) Parents' involvement in their children's learning, Paper for the 7th Early Childhood Convention, N.Z. Pen Green Conference.

Whalley, M. (ed.) and the Pen Green Centre Team (1997) *Working with Parents*. London: Hodder and Stoughton.

Whalley, M. (ed.) and the Pen Green Centre Team (2001) *Involving Parents in their Children's Learning*. London: Paul Chapman Publishing.

Winnicott, D.W. (1964) *The Child, the Family, and the Outside World*. London and Melbourne: Penguin.

Winnicott, D.W. (1991) *Playing and Reality*. London and New York: Routledge.

Woodhead, M., Faulkner, D. and Littleton, K. (1998) *Cultural Worlds of Early Childhood*. London and New York: Routledge and the Open University.

Young, S. (2003) *Music with the Under Fours*. London and New York: Routledge Falmer.

# INDEX